Neoliberal Africa

About the author

GRAHAM HARRISON teaches politics at the University of Sheffield. He has written on democratisation, corruption, governance and the World Bank, with a particular interest in Africa and especially eastern Africa. He is an editor of *New Political Economy* and is coordinating editor of *Review of African Political Economy*.

Neoliberal Africa

The impact of global social engineering

GRAHAM HARRISON

Zed Books

LONDON & NEW YORK

Neoliberal Africa: The Impact of Global Social Engineering was first published
in 2010 by Zed Books Ltd, 7 Cynthia Street, London N1 9JF, UK
and Room 400, 175 Fifth Avenue, New York, NY 10010, USA

www.zedbooks.co.uk

Copyright © Graham Harrison 2010

The right of Graham Harrison to be identified as the author
of this work has been asserted by him in accordance with
the Copyright, Designs and Patents Act, 1988

FSC

Mixed Sources
Product group from well-managed
forests and other controlled sources

Cert no. SGS-COC-002953
www.fsc.org
© 1996 Forest Stewardship Council

Typeset in Monotype Bulmer
by illuminati, Grosmont
Index by John Barker
Cover designed by Safehouse Creative
Printed and bound in Great Britain by
CPI Antony Rowe, Chippenham and Eastbourne

Distributed in the USA exclusively by Palgrave Macmillan, a division of
St Martin's Press, LLC, 175 Fifth Avenue, New York, NY 10010, USA

A catalogue record for this book is available from the British Library
Library of Congress Cataloging in Publication Data available

ISBN 978 1 84813 319 8 Hb
ISBN 978 1 84813 320 4 Pb
ISBN 978 1 84813 321 1 Eb

Contents

I

Neoliberalism in Africa, neoliberalism and Africa

Africa at the forefront

[Africa] has been thrust into modern world history in incontrovertibly powerful and long-lasting ways. The slave and tropical commodity trades changed the world, industrial and non-industrial alike. The recalcitrance of European theory in the face of Africa is a construct of the same history, a co-production of Africa and Europe over centuries of economic and political engagement. (Guyer 2004: 14)

Lagos is not catching up with us. Rather, we may be catching up with Lagos. (Koolhaas et al. in Ferguson 2007: 75)

I T IS commonplace to find passing references to Africa (in this book meaning south of the Sahara) as a 'switched off' place in the global political economy. Indeed, some major and excellent volumes on global neoliberalism simply ignore Africa (Campbell and Pedersen 2001; Soederberg et al. 2005). It is for this reason that David Moore rightly states that 'studies of globalisation often ignore, or provide only passing coverage of, Africa' (2001: 909; see also Brown 2006). This ignorance is not just an expression of the alignment of international studies with the structuring of economic and state power and Western predominance (Hobson and Seabrook 2007; Engel and Rye Olsen 2005); it is also a product of the arguments and reflections of many scholars who are particularly interested in Africa (for an illustrative set of examples, see Sender 1999: 89–90; for the orthodox view, see Nissanke and Thorbecke 2008: 1). In the West more generally, Africa is represented in the media and mainstream culture as remote, exceptional and characterised as lacking to some degree or other the proper properties held by the 'international community' or 'globalisation' (Elbadawi and Sambanis 2000: 245; Werbner and Ranger 1996). In broad sweep, and not without a little licence for flair of expression, Achille Mbembe makes a striking summary:

> Africa ... is portrayed as a vast dark cave where every benchmark and distinction come together in total confusion, and the rifts of tragic and unhappy human history stand revealed; a mixture of the half-created and the incomplete, strange signs, compulsive movements, in short a bottomless abyss where everything is noise, yawning gaps and primordial chaos. (2001: 3)

There is a lot to take in and unpack here, but it is difficult to disagree with the import of this overview: public and popular cultures in the West tend to represent Africa in terms of absences, delinquencies or alienness – each of which serves to reinforce a sense of Africa's marginality from any sense of global convergence and/or progress.

The robustness of this general trope is all the more striking for the fact that it has persisted throughout a period in which another discourse, that of globalisation, has worked to represent the world as increasingly interconnected and converging (Rupert 2000; Hay and Marsh 1999). Discursively, talk of globalisation can be understood as a recent and virulent incarnation of an expansive liberalism (Hovden and Keene 2001) which aims to encapsulate national, cultural and economic differences as ephemeral: either as differences that *don't* make a difference, as 'historically contingent' (Tsakalotos 2005: 894) or as 'rigidities and vestiges' (Bourdieu 1998) that temporarily encumber liberal realisations. Within this view,

Homo economicus is seen as the originary state of the human being. In other words, socio-economic diversity does not undermine the notion – or faith (Weis 2004: 462; Geschiere and Nyamnjoh 2000: 444; Marangos 2008: 238, and especially Comaroff and Comaroff 2000) – that there is a deeper global logic of convergence towards a particular form of sociability. That form of sociability is based in two lodestones: the free market and the rational individual (Williams 1999; Vlachou and Christou 1999: 2; Tsakalotos 2004: 10ff.). It is worth noting that neoliberal ideas frame rationality in a specific fashion – individualised, utilitarian and egoistic – which by no means exhausts ontologies of rationality (Manor 1991: 311).

It is this sociability – and the premiss that this is a foundational or essential human sociability – that allows globalisation discourse to imagine a converging humanity without articulating any significant aspects of coercion or severe disruption but rather as a positive-sum, consensual and stable process. The 'challenges', 'issues' and 'problems' with globalisation in this liberal view are second-order, concerning reform scheduling and design (Sachs 2005; Stiglitz 2007), the pace and nature of market-led modernisation (Easterly 2007; de Soto 2001), or the means to deal with 'externalities' such as environmental damage. In sum, a powerful discourse of globalisation has emerged in the last twenty years which projects a global process of integration and harmonisation – convergence – which is in all societies' interests.

These two discourses – of African exceptionalism and liberal integrative globalisation – produce a dissonance: an awkwardly conjoined sense of the universal and the particular in which Africa's place in any narrative of globalisation is significantly underspecified compared with other world regions. Nevertheless, some account of Africa must be made in order for those who advocate the liberal globalising canon to claim a universal worldview. This account creates a global cognitive landscape in which 'globalisation is passing Africa by', Africa is not fully globalised, and analogous phrases. This is often the metaphor evoked in IMF communications. Consider the following text specifically addressed to the 'Challenges of Globalisation for Africa': 'countries that fail to participate in this trend toward integration run the risk of being left behind' (Ouattara 1997). The effects of this discursive confluence are at best misleading and at worst pernicious. This book argues that if we move beyond liberal globalisation ideology, we can see that Africa is as much at the heart of globalisation as any other place.

Africa is at the *forefront* of a globalised project of neoliberal reform. We will come to reflect in detail on the definition and meaning of neoliberalism, but let us start with a representative and encompassing description: 'neoliberalism is a theory of political economic practices proposing that human well-being can best be advanced by the maximisation of entrepreneurial freedoms within an institutional framework characterised by private property rights, individual liberty, unencumbered markets, and free trade.' (Harvey 2007: 22). If we understand a key facet of globalisation as the 'rolling out' of neoliberalism (Peck and Tickell 2002), then we should acknowledge that any proper study of neoliberalism as a globalising project should locate Africa at the heart of its research because it is a world region that has undergone such extensive and protracted neoliberal social engineering (Kozul-Wright and Rayment 2007: 177). Furthermore, the fortunes of neoliberalism in Africa are instructive for how we understand neoliberalism in other places and how we understand globalisation more broadly. To understand neoliberal globalisation, Africa provides vital insights and lessons (most of them cautionary) for the rest of the world. This is the point of departure for this book, and it is from here that we will consider the protracted neoliberal project in Africa as a form of global social engineering.

Africa/globalisation

There is something rather rehearsed about discussing the definition of globalisation, so I will try to dispense with it quickly here in order to push the narrative forward. Globalisation simply speaks to the increasing interconnectedness between and beyond states that is driven by capital and its increasing concentration and mobility. There is a lot one might debate here, but globalisation debates have proven to be unending and this definition is not exceptionally controversial, so it can reasonably serve to shape the points made in this section.

If it is misleading to think of Africa as outside of/remote from globalisation then we must consider not only the ways in which Africa is globalised but also how Africa, in its relations with other places, produces globalisation (see also Moore 2001: 909). James Ferguson speaks of Africa's 'place in the world' (2006), arguing that many African states have been through a broadly similar experience of stalled national modernisation followed by externally led processes of neoliberal reform, or what he revealingly calls 'scientific capitalism' (1995). In other words, these authors rightly emphasise not any putative remoteness from globalisation but the problematic nature of Africa's terms of engagement with globalisation.

This book takes this point of departure to argue that Africa's 'connectivity' is not just important per se; that is, in terms of how Africa is affected by economic integration. Additionally, Africa's globalisation is part of globalisation in a more generic sense. We are interested not simply in Africa's globalisation but also in Africa/globalisation. This might initially appear to be a semantic nicety, but the distinction has important cognitive repercussions. It collapses the enduring dualism that persists between Africa and a external putative 'globalisation', and it compels us to recognise that – however we understand it – globalisation is as much composed of the political economy of change in Africa as it is any other region. To borrow from Jane Guyer's eloquent words which started this chapter, Africa and globalisation are co-produced.

A further repercussion of this conceptual and semantic shift is political. If we are concerned to challenge and critically evaluate the more apologistic narratives on globalisation, we should be ready to challenge the ideological effects of a globalisation–Africa dualism in which many of the most damaging, regressive and ugly aspects of globalisation are (dis)placed into Africa in order to represent them as manifestations of recidivism, anachronism and deviance. On the contrary: mass poverty, 'surplus' populations, state collapse, and other features of Africa's development crisis are at the heart of globalisation. To locate them as residual phenomena – 'more bad news from Africa' – is ideologically to dissemble a fuller understanding of global capitalism in the service of more bourgeois or romantic projections of globalisation.

Economic fragility

The Africa/globalisation frame of reference might usefully reject the neat dualisms of the mainstream contra divergent, or progressive contra delinquent, but it does leave us with an awkwardness in understanding Africa as a specific world-region which is in some sense specific; not just like anywhere else. We will return to this question of Africa's *differentia specifica* throughout the book. Here, our starting point is to recognise that certain facets of global capitalism, although generic, have been more emphatically embodied in African sovereignties.

If there is one key phrase to introduce these particular manifestations of generic aspects of global capitalism it is 'combined and uneven development'. The tendencies to integrate all spaces into global capitalism has produced within Africa modern forms of economic fragility and spatial differentiation, the disintegrative effects of which are mediated through the regulative processes of the state system, albeit one structured by massive inequalities of power.

With regard to the first theme – economic fragility – it is important to acknowledge that Africa contains a very high proportion of small and vulnerable economies. Many states rely on a limited number of primary exports whose prices have been generally falling and/or unstable (Gibbon and Ponte 2005). These exports are then processed, used in manufacture, and embedded into technologies outside Africa so that the 'downstream' value is realised elsewhere. Where African countries have manufactured and exported goods, recent changes in the global economy have rendered these exports similar to primary commodities (Kaplinski 2005): low unstable prices and intense competition for consumer markets have made low-technology manufacturing less of a 'take-off' sector than it was perceived to be in the 1960s and 1970s when development economists saw this as a *sine qua non* for economic growth.

This is not to argue that African economies are populated by subsistence farmers who suffer a disconnection from modern markets and whose sole vulnerability comes from variable rainfall. Rather, and in broad brushstrokes, African agrarian livelihoods are defined by a range of unstable and largely unrewarding engagements with broader market relations. Households in the main rely on some combination of trade, agriculture and wage labour – formal or informal, more or less secure – in order to reproduce themselves (Bernstein 2004). These multiplex livelihoods (Bryceson et al. 2000) create 'modern' and integrated forms of poverty, an outcome not solely of low technology in agriculture but also of low wages, and low and unstable prices for goods sold (whether crops or artisanal goods) (Cramer et al. 2008). They also produce dynamic forms of social differentiation (Ponte 2001) and break down reified distinctions between the urban and the rural. Nevertheless, it remains the case that the internally complex tapestries of rural livelihoods in Africa encompass economies which produce little income, a slender tax base, and unstable and meagre processes of accumulation (Ellis 2000).

Although it is a fair generalisation to say that African economies are small and fragile, this is not to say that globalisation has not happened in Africa; rather, it is to say that the interactions between African economies and international/transnational economic flows are highly unequal. In a nutshell, Africa's influence over the broad patterns of international political economy is slight, but shifts and changes in the latter make a great deal of difference to the former.

The politics of international debt provide a rough and ready diagnostic of Africa's economic vulnerability. A slightly dated but illustrative example of this is the debt crisis that emerged in the early 1980s. In 1982/3, the failure of Brazil and Mexico to maintain payments on debt to the World Bank and the IMF triggered a series of responses by the Bretton Woods institutions, the American government, and other institutions to reschedule, open new lines of credit, and try to secure currency stability in the large but highly indebted economies of Latin America. During the same period, similar degrees of debt peonage in small African economies barely registered on the world stage: instead, the World Bank and the IMF were given pretty much an autonomous remit to implement economic conditionalities on distressed economies whilst debt was managed (not often reduced) by the World Bank, the IMF and the Paris Club of bilateral donors. For the US Treasury, the international economic think-tanks, banks, investors and financial journalists, economic meltdown in African states mattered little.

A related example can be found in a more recent comparison with Southeast Asia, which accrued large amounts of debt during the 1990s. Nevertheless, whereas most African countries had a debt-to-export ratio of about 200 per cent, the proportions in Southeast Asia were significantly lower: 34 per cent in Malaysia and 78 per cent in Thailand (African Development Bank 2006: 13).

These two regional comparisons reveal how international debt serves as a diagnostic of the political economy of Africa's economic fragility. In the first case, we saw how extremely debt-distressed African economies merited only the most meagre 'rescue packages', executed through the World Bank and the IMF and attached to punitive conditionalities (see Chapters 2 and 4) because these economies were of only marginal importance to the 'core' regions of global capitalism. In the second example, we saw how large amounts of international debt are not straightforwardly a problem and that the accrual of debt during sustained economic growth can in fact be beneficial. Indebtedness in Africa reveals the smallness of African national economies and their generally disappointing rates of economic growth (with some exceptions in the first decade of this century) – both core features of Africa's economic fragility. The particular vulnerability of Africa has only worsened since the 1990s: by the turn of the century, Africa had 5 per cent of developing countries' income and two-thirds of its debt (Prempeh 2006: 141).

This is a core motif of Africa's place within globalisation: more than any other region in the world, Africa represents and exemplifies the salience of the radically uneven and unequal contours of globalisation. Concentrations of capital, wealth and a highly unequal state system all render globalisation as something that is by and large 'done to' Africa. So much for liberal notions of convergence, positive-sum outcomes, and the beneficial effects of competition.

Spatial segmentation

The second theme refers to what Frederick Cooper has characterised as the 'lumpy' nature of investment in Africa (2001), or what a previous generation of radical scholars called 'enclave' development. That is to say, most of the flows of investment into Africa tend to focus on very specific and often spatially fixed opportunities in which the primary aim is the quick and efficient evacuation of a commodity rather than any broader engagement with national manufacturers, suppliers or consumer markets.

Throughout the 1990s, principal examples of this could be found in the vegetable and cut-flower sectors. In countries such as Kenya and Zimbabwe, out-of-season high-value vegetables and flowers could be grown in irrigated and chemically managed fields and greenhouses, then chilled and carried by air freight to the large supermarket purchasers or to European agricultural markets. These sectors have grown rapidly, but have employed small numbers of low-skilled (often female) workers in the most labour-intensive and low-paid jobs – for example US$40 equivalent per month in Kenya.

In the 2000s, as mineral prices rose, other enclaves have emerged, especially around oil reserves and most notably the Bight of Benin. Again, similar issues have surfaced concerning the broader impact of oil exploitation on 'host' societies. The most prominent example here is the Delta region in Nigeria (Frynas 1998). Since the execution of Ken Saro-Wiwa by the Nigerian government, the region has remained unstable and the oil companies effectively 'gated communities' of installations and expatriate personnel.

The cloistered and securitised nature of mineral investment is present *in extremis* in those countries suffering some form of civil conflict, prominent examples being the Democratic Republic of Congo and Sudan. In regards to high-value minerals (or rising value minerals such as copper was until 2007), investment is secured through the more-or-less transparent co-option of local brokers to provide a requisite security to the investment. This might give rise to partnerships with state-owned or local private mineral companies, or the bringing in of wealthy and powerful Africans to management boards. Beyond this, a minimal level of low-level employment and a system of pipelines and transport routes represents the extent of connection with the rest of the country (see the Chad–Cameroon oil pipeline, for example).

Existing evidence suggests that newer geographies of foreign direct investment (FDI) – deriving largely from China but also India, Malaysia and others – do not significantly move beyond the focus on mineral enclaves and the desire to evacuate these minerals to serve processes of accumulation elsewhere (Tull 2006). Nevertheless, investment – direct and indirect (in the form of credit and aid) from these 'Asian drivers' has attained immense significance in some countries, which opens up possibilities of less neoliberal modalities of aid, investment and trade (Brautigam 2003, especially on Mauritius).

This second theme shows how globalisation has followed socio-spatial inequalities that have frequently been historically integral to the colonial and post-colonial project of state construction. It shows how Africa's engagement with international capital has produced spatial differentiation and disintegration to such a degree that it has become almost impossible to 'capture' the value produced by FDI within a national space in ways that might serve to finance a programme of national development.

Taken together, we can characterise Africa as manifesting particular aspects of globalisation more strongly than other regions. The economic/spatial unevenness and unequal structuring of the international state system intrinsic to globalisation are revealed to us most clearly in Africa.

Globalised regulation

Thus far, we have looked at the key patterns of Africa's economic engagement with the global political economy. But this only takes us so far. All aspects of 'economic' globalisation are in fact more properly understood politically as well as economically. Separating the political and the economic might be useful for analytical purposes, but to suppose that there is a phenomenon called 'the market' which operates solely according to the laws of supply and demand is at best a useful abstraction and we should be very cautious as to how we use it. For our purposes, it is important to note that Africa's economic fragility is integrated into – and expressed through – its experience of statehood.

Let us start with some general coordinates before we move on to some more empirically specific material. Modern African states were created during the late stages of European colonialism. African colonial states were designed for imperial purposes and more generally with the grandeur of the empire in mind. Consequently, statehood – if it can be called that – emerged rapidly and from outside to impose alien rule; to create conduits for the export of commodities to Europe; to deny, erase or incorporate; and to impose a racially defined order to 'civilisation' upon Africans whatever their culture, class or gender (Freund 1998; Davidson 1992; Boone 2003) or existing forms of power. This was the highly problematic context within which independence was won, mainly in the 1960s, and it left newly established ruling classes with states that were locked in to a Western-centred global political economy, inheriting a tense relationship with their national societies (Clapham 1996; Mamdani 1996). Post-colonial political trajectories have been diverse and profound, creating a divergence away from colonial templates (Young 2004). Nevertheless, it would be difficult to identify among these diverse post-colonial histories a clear example of an African state that has escaped a strong subordination to Western states without running the risk of state instability and/or mass violence. This historically constructed condition is central to any understanding of Africa/globalisation.

The shaping of African sovereignties within a global states system filters through all manner of more specific social and economic connections. Here, we will briefly review aspects of economic interaction to highlight the nature of external control, and also to foreshadow the global impetus of neoliberal reforms.

Intergovernmental trade reforms have been a pivotal part of Africa's changing trading relations: the entire raft of trade preferences constructed through the Lomé Agreements has (with varying degrees of support for African states) tied African trade to Europe. Right now, African regions are embarking on the implementation of economic partnership agreements (EPAs) which will likely lock African economies into static comparative advantages vis-à-vis Europe, leading towards an end to preferences within fifteen years. In regard to specific commodities, some African countries have participated in the politics of WTO agreements concerning the legality and legitimacy of trade support and liberalisation, for example in sugar (Gibb 2004).

These examples show how trade liberalisation is not simply the removal of quotas (all but extinguished) and tariffs (constantly ratcheted down). Trade liberalisation is also enacted through international and regional agreement; it involves trade diplomacy, reform scheduling, the categorisation of commodities, the construction of 'open regionalism' (Gamble and Payne 1996), and it is underpinned by aid and loan programmes that promote trade liberalisation.

And trade liberalisation is only one case in point: aid, international finance and foreign direct investment (FDI) are all structured through inter-state politics as well. International aid is constitutive of African states – it is part of states' development policy; it is a material relation that underpins (unequal) relations between states; and it produces discourses of intervention, monitoring and diplomacy. This is institutionalised through 'Paris Club' donor meetings, G8 annual meetings, various 'Consensus' agreements, the OECD (and especially the Paris Declaration), and a wide variety of donor groups and subgroups in each country (for a good overview, see Callaghy 2002).

But it is also the case that finance and investment are integrated into interactions between states. Most development finance for Africa derives from the World Bank and the IMF, which are intergovernmental organisations (IGOs), profoundly based in the historical dominance of the West and especially the United States (Wade 2002). FDI flows are more complex, but are certainly infused with state politics, with states acting as supports or promoters of international investment flows (which are still largely nationally based even if globally dispersed), or as gatekeepers setting conditions for investment inflow. The World Bank and the IMF have their own instruments to support companies investing in Africa and elsewhere (the Multilateral Investment Guarantee Agency MIGA and the International Finance Corporation IFC within the World Bank) (see Bracking 2009). The World Bank's ICSID offers arbitration services for disputes concerning foreign investment – largely in favour of capital rather than states (*Bretton Woods Update* 56: 6), and a welter of investment promotion agencies has emerged – again to promote the institutionalisation of capital-friendly regulation (Phelps et al. 2007: 87). A great deal of the FDI that has entered Africa in the last twenty years has developed on the back of strong pressures by Western states (and IGOs) to privatise public utilities and state-owned enterprises and to set up international tenders for transfer of ownership (Bayliss and Hall 2002, Smith 2005). More opaquely, FDI is often accompanied by bribery and extra-economic bargaining and pressurising that might involve governments – both Western and African (Bracking 2001). The rise in Chinese investment into Africa might suggest different models of investment modality but it also emphasises again the centrality of the state to the shaping of international investment deal brokering.

This book will be looking at a broader range of political practices which it defines collectively as neoliberal reform. There are, of course, a lot of points that need to be clarified before we can proceed to map and evaluate this project of neoliberal social engineering. The rest of this introductory chapter will deal with these before setting out how the rest of the book will proceed.

Africa/globalisation: key features

Loxley and Sackey argue that, 'though diverse structures exist among African countries, there are sufficient basic features common to countries on the continent to make a macroeconomic study involving all of them' (2008: 163–4). The authors do not go on to specify what these common features might be, but the assumption that they make is a common one in economics, and to a large extent other social sciences as well. There are certainly some very general common historical and economic features that pertain to Africa that are essentially the result of a late and brutal European colonisation, namely: the construction of the basic sinews of the state over or upon existing political geographies (Boone 2003; Herbst 2000), the forging of settler and export sectors which served European states (Freund 1988), forms of indirect rule (Mamdani 1996), and a piecemeal attempt at cultural imposition which is perhaps most salient in the hegemonic status of European languages throughout Africa (with some exceptions, e.g. kiSwahili in Tanzania). But the homogenising effects of colonialism, which was based on crude templates devised largely by Britain, France and Portugal, does not get us that far. For one thing, no colonial power succeeded in erasing pre-existing social dynamics. Fluid and diverse social relations endured, adapted, resisted and even flourished under those aspects of European rule that they encountered. Thus, pre-existing diversities – although hardly unchanging – persisted throughout and beyond the colonial interlude (Bayart 1991). Furthermore, the influence and effects of colonialism have been extremely varied throughout post-colonial Africa. Also, the sense that African states were a product of a colonial legacy might have been convincing in the late 1960s, but the strength of this argument is less apparent after forty or fifty years of independence, however dominant external forces might have been throughout (Young 2004).

Thus, beyond the broadest of sweeps, it is difficult to speak of Africa as a coherent historical social entity. One way of enhancing Africa as a category is to highlight its politically constructed nature, what Mamdani refers to as Africa as a 'unity' (1995). This might be taken in two ways, one weak and one strong. The weak approach would be to emphasise the ways in which African states have integrated with each other or acted globally as a collective. The evidence here is extremely limited. The history of the Organisation of African Unity is of a weak regional organisation that concerned itself with the maintenance of post-colonial sovereignties rather than regional integration or international collective action (Clapham 1996). Subregional integration has made more progress in some places, but the complexities and diversities in this area add as much to the notion of difference within the continent as they do to its unity. This is no less the case today as it was when subregional organisations were established in the 1960s and 1970s.

The stronger approach would be to concentrate on the discursive deployment of Africa as a category. The premiss here is that whatever empirical commonalities one might wish to identify across the continent, the coherence of Africa derives mainly from its political and discursive construction. Africa might be constructed negatively through processes of 'othering' (Chabal 1992), as indeed is the case in many Western cultures, frequently relying on racial tropes of primitivism and indolence (Nederveen Pieterse 1992). Africa might also be constructed positively through assertions of value against imperial derogations. A key aspect of this is Afrocentrism, a politics and culture constructed to demonstrate and promote a belief in African ideas and sociability (Asante 2007). This Africa discourse has been produced by African intellectuals but also in various diasporas, especially by Afro-American intellectuals (Howe 1998). As such, Africa's unity is constructed ideationally and transnationally (Appiah 1993). In all of these settings, Africa's unity, its status as a social entity, is contingent on its discursive production and reproduction rather than any positivist common features shared between countries.

This book relies on the premiss that we can meaningfully speak about Africa. We can do this without needing definitively to establish an African 'essence', a *differentia specifica*, that renders the continent a single entity. Indeed the gist of this book is to argue that Africa is extreme not exceptional: it manifests the most radical instances of a generic aspect of contemporary globalisation – that is, neoliberal reform. So, in what sense can we speak of 'Africa'?

Recalling the Loxley and Sackey quotation, it is noteworthy that, although they do not elaborate the 'common features' of Africa, they do say that these common features allow a specific kind of enquiry to take place: of political economy. Implicitly, the point is that the way and extent to which one can speak of Africa depend in part on the kind of issue that one is interested in. To research African *culture* would indeed be a complex and hazardous line of enquiry. To look at development policy and its impacts – especially during a period in which external actors have been so powerful – seems to me an altogether more secure way to approach Africa as a whole (Round 2007). Here, one can analyse an extant continental–global set of interactions, whilst also maintaining an awareness and respect for national socio-cultural diversities in more specific instances. This is the approach that this book will take.

Indeed, the assumption that Africa has a particular set of development issues, problems and requisite solutions is so prominent within international development that it shapes the practice of development and neoliberal interventions (see Williams 2008: 69). The World Bank (the major prosecutor of neoliberal reform within the continent) produces periodic reports on Africa as a region, constructing an empirically rich discourse of Africa as a single space with particular development issues – largely defined through an absence of the requisite properties for development or through crisis (World Bank 1989, 2000a). Much of the Bank's development practice is 'Africa specific' – an early example being the setting up of the Special Office for African Affairs in 1984, a recent example being the Africa Results Monitoring System in 2007. The United Nations family of development organisations, along with bilateral development ministries and departments, routinely categorise Africa in regionally specific terms. Academics, consultants and think-tanks often rely upon the same cognitive geography. And, to a large degree, this categorisation is based on shared characterisations of Africa: as exceptionally poor, exceptionally agrarian, exceptionally unstable, and exceptionally backward. As ever in development discourse and practice, problems and solutions are mutually defining (Mosse 2005). The problems – often empirically substantiated – are couched in ways that articulate solutions in the form of development interventions. Discourse produces practice and vice versa. Within this discursive and practical traffic Africa is represented and acted upon.

This reform project is based in an economistic core belief in the free market and (near) perfect competition, but it is – like the examples given above – pursued through state action and most notably the interventions of Western states and IGOs in African development policymaking. It is the argument of this book that Africa/globalisation is centrally a story of neoliberal global social engineering: a project to envision, compel, encourage and socialise African states into a trajectory of marketisation. The aim of this book is to detail this project in its full complexity, and to demonstrate both its substantive failures as a development strategy and its limits as an emerging form of social practice.

Introducing neoliberalism

This is where neoliberalism makes its entrée. In 1981 the World Bank published a research report titled *Accelerated Development in Sub-Saharan Africa: An Agenda to Action*, commonly known as the Berg Report. The report is best known for its attack on post-colonial African states and its recommendation for the removal of government from the economy, but it also takes a good number of pages to portray an African developmental malaise, shared by states across the continent. The Berg Report contrives a particular account of crisis, based in manifold causes – internal structural constraints, natural resources, population growth (a World Bank mainstay), and damaging state action. It goes on to pose that domestic policy and institutional reform are the key to economic recovery, with a far slighter emphasis on international global economic change; and these policy reforms are largely driven at the rolling back of the state from economic management.

The period from 1979 to 1981 is commonly understood as the birth of neoliberalism as a global policy raft and political ideology. At that time, it was *only* in regard to Africa that a region-wide representation of statist problems and marketised solutions was propounded. In other words, one of the most powerful discursive constructions of Africa – and certainly one that has endured to the present day – is of a continent that has failed to produce 'proper' market economies, or to have 'neoliberalised'. Subsequent World Bank reports in 1989 and 1994 reiterate the basic problematic, and the 'development community' has aligned itself with this vision. 'Special funds' for Africa to facilitate neoliberal transformation have been commonplace and a great swathe of conditionality, policy advice, aid and technical assistance have focused specifically on Africa to engineer neoliberal reform, all of which we will look at in later chapters.

Thus far, this chapter has set out an orienting frame to understand Africa/globalisation and neoliberalism. Africa, I have argued, is not exceptional to a globalising trend; rather, it manifests specific aspects of globalisation in extreme form and these specific aspects can be usefully bundled together under the rubric 'neoliberalism'. In this sense, I have suggested, studying Africa is not a study in deviance or backwardness but in fact a study of 'cutting edge' or most contemporary neoliberalism-in-practice. The datum for this story is 1981, but since then Africa has undergone an expanding remit of neoliberal reform, championed by key international agencies.

All of which leads us to an obvious and important question: what is neoliberalism? The answer to this is apparently straightforward but in fact rather intriguing. Almost all work on neoliberalism converges around a core definitional syllogism: the fundamental political good is freedom of the individual, which is best secured through a competitive market society, which in turn is only possible in states that do not interfere in the economy beyond that which is strictly necessary to ensure the second condition (see Hay 2004: 507–8; Overbeek and van der Pijl 1993: 15). It is, then, a contemporary social project based in neoclassical economics or liberal social theory – hence the *neo*liberal epithet. In this straightforward sense, neoliberalism might be thought of as an academic synonym of more straightforward terms such as laissez-faire, marketisation, or rolling back the state.

There is also a commonly accepted historical narrative that explains the political emergence of neoliberalism. Here, as already stated, the late 1970s and early 1980s are pivotal. This is the period in which economic crisis in specific developed capitalist states, and an enduring global slow-down, created political opportunities for 'new right' parties and intellectuals to gain ground (England and Ward 2002: 249–50; Craig and Cotterell 2007). In the United Kingdom the Conservative Party and Margaret Thatcher, in the USA the Republicans under Ronald Reagan, and in (then) West Germany under Helmut Kohl, public policy actively sought to remove direct state involvement in the economy, to reduce social subsidies and expenditure (at least in some areas), and to undermine the political power of organised labour and other progressive political organisations in favour of capital, or factions within this class (Dumeil and Levy 2004). Economic liberalism was the 'crisis defining idea' (Blyth 2007: 762) that defined policy responses to economic slowdown and class struggle.

As these specific political-economic shifts were under way in some of the core states of the global political economy, international organisations – most crucially the World Bank and IMF – started to articulate a revived advocacy of the market as the institution that would promote development. Indeed, during the 1980s, especially for the IMF, 'development' became a synonym for marketisation (Rapley 2002, Leys 1996, Brohman 2005c). The whole edifice of development throughout the post-war period, based in structural differences between the 'First' and 'Third' worlds, was conflated into a unified representation of the world's states as all converging towards a single market transition. In Thomas Friedman's words: 'today there is no more First World ... Third World. There's just the Fast World – the world of the wide-open plain – and the Slow World' (Friedman 2000: 46). Development was simply 'economic evolution' in the words of the WTO's first president (Michael Moore in McMichael 2000: 472), or, more elaborately:

> The rules that apply in Latin America or Eastern Europe apply in India as well ... [Third World countries] need to understand that there is no longer such a thing as separate and distinct Indian econo-

mies ... there is just economics. (Larry Summers, former World
Bank Chief Economist, in George and Sabelli 1994: 106)

Throughout the 1980s, and with increasing confidence, these
international organisations pursued global economic convergence
based on the free-market model. So, why create a neologism to
define this overt and well-defended project? Why not simply call
it liberalisation? Here we come to a more contested and politicised
terrain: 'neoliberalism' is a term infused with normative import.
There are few self-confessed neoliberals; it is a term devised by the
political left to develop critiques of the market project, a 'radical-
theoretical slogan' (Peck 2004: 403). In this sense, it is the *naming*
that matters: it assigns to an institution or individual a critical view
of their actions. But, even if it has radical import, 'neoliberalism'
remains an open text: it has generated a variety of interpretations.
We can, however, map these fairly easily.

Procrustean development

This critical approach emphasises neoliberalism's 'flat' social
imagery (Soderberg 2002a). The argument here is that neoliberalism 'sees' societies as economies and considers the extent to which
they conform to an open and competitive market model which
serves as the monadic reference-point for all societies. Neoliberalism imagines the world in its own image: open, market-conforming
economies based in liberal societies. Neoliberalism aims 'to build
a universe out of aggregated transactions' (Comaroff and Comaroff
2000: 305).

In this sense, neoliberalism 'virtually abolishes the idea of
development as a specific concern, in favour of a universal set
of prescriptions applied to developed and developing economies
alike' (Cammack 2002: 159). As such, one critique based in the
concept of neoliberalism is that which contests the one-model-for-
all approach to development. This is expressed most strongly in
institutionalist and post-Keynesian political economy (Chang 2002)
in which the alternative premiss is that successful development

requires economic policy unorthodoxy, something that neoliberalism is innately hostile to as it closes down 'development space'
(Wade 2003).

Neoliberal imperialism

Closely related to the first approach is a critique based in an
awareness of the Western origins of neoliberalism. Recognising
neoliberalism's 'flat' world-view, this perspective aims to identify
a 'core' interest or aggregated agency pushing this model. It is
here that neoliberalism becomes a specifically Western project, or
sometimes an American one (Chomsky 1998; Nederveen Pieterse
2004; Panitch and Konings 2009). There are two cardinal repercussions within this approach: firstly, neoliberalism is imposed on
the post-colonial and former Communist world. This means that
neoliberalism involves the more or less forced opening up of non-
Western economies to Western influence, and it means an attempt
to impose Western models of society on the diversity of social
forms throughout the rest of the world. John Brohman argues that
neoliberalism is fundamentally Eurocentric and is based on an
assumption that all societies are constituted by rational modern
individuals along the lines of *Homo economicus*, the classic image
of the self created by European liberal political economy (Brohman
1995a, 1995b). It is in this sense that neoliberalism appears as the
most recent in a longer tradition of imperialism, an imperialism
defined by the projection of the political good – whether called
'civilisation', 'development' or 'good governance' – from the West
onto other parts of the world. Neoliberalism is one more project
in a programme of Western imposition that commenced with
colonisation (Cooke 2003; Kothari and Minogue 1988).

Second, the 'imperial' imposition of neoliberalism on the
non-West leaves open the possibility that neoliberalism is not a
universal template, but rather a differentiated project to maintain a
global system of core and periphery. In other words, neoliberalism
might be an effective way of intervening and dominating post-

colonial and post-Communist countries, but it is not necessarily
to be taken seriously in regard to Western states' governance or
economic policy. Some authors have argued that this has produced
a globalised double standard – of market fundamentalism for the
non-West and an enduring unorthodoxy, protectionism and even
mercantilism in the West (Harvey 2007; Harman 2008).

Disciplinary neoliberalism

We have already seen that the neoliberal project is hardly short on
ambition. Indeed, it is represented by some as a tectonic change in
the way that the world works. For some critiques, this is the heart
of the matter of neoliberalism: its ability to produce global power
and order. Perhaps the definitive place to start here is with Stephen
Gill's well-known article 'Globalisation, Market Civilisation, and
Disciplinary Neoliberalism' (1995). The key point is the phrase
disciplinary neoliberalism: Gill argues that neoliberal reforms
require invigilation, and where reforms become skewed 'remedial'
mechanisms are required. These might involve punitive measures
such as the cutting of credit lines, the downgrading of a country
in one of the manifold economic country rankings (investment
security, economic stability, policy indicators, corruption indicators, risk indicators), or the cutting of development aid.

Thus neoliberalism is, in this view, best understood as a global
'architecture' of authority and material power which can both
incentivise and punish divergence and reform 'slippage'. In this
perspective, the prominence of the World Bank, the IMF and the
World Trade Organisation (WTO) within international regulation
and liberalisation is key (Soederberg 2002b), as is the network of
private and quasi-private network of banks, credit-rating agencies,
and standards agencies. It is in this respect that Chorev sees the
WTO as a key 'institutional project' in neoliberal globalisation
(2005). Regional agreements based on open market economic
integration ('open regionalism') provide further evidence of this
neoliberal architecture in construction (Lee and McBride 2007).

Although Gill wrote from a Marxist/Gramscian perspective, the notion of discipline has also been extensively elaborated by those writing in a Foucauldian tradition, paying special attention to Foucault's work on discipline in modern European states. Neoliberalism is seen as a discursive and normalising power which shapes conformity to a market model. The key Foucauldian concept here is governmentality, which leads some to see neoliberalism as a discourse to 'facilitate the governing of individuals from a distance' (Larner 2000: 6) by shaping subjectivities. Neoliberalism discursively produces subjectivities of individualised entrepreneurialism, which, whilst not necessarily being subject to large amounts of state authority, are subjects of market governmentality within all social realms – incentivised workers, consumers, citizens, entrepreneurs and so on.

Another of the key ways in which neoliberal governmentality works is by removing contentious political aspects of reform from public remit by rendering them as either entirely necessary and unavoidable ('there is no alternative') or as technical or scientific aspects of policymaking (recall Ferguson's term 'scientific capitalism'). The collective noun for these acts is depoliticisation, and it constitutes the heart of the discursive power of neoliberalism (Harriss 2002; Kamat 2004: 167–70) because it stymies opposition to neoliberalism by labelling political resistance as 'factionalism' or self-seeking 'pressure group activity' (Cohen and Rogers 1992; Beckman 1993). A substantial debt is owed to the secular book *The Anti-Politics Machine* by James Ferguson (1994), which is centrally concerned not with neoliberalism but rather with development agencies more generally and their inability to encompass specific aspects of Lesotho's political economy into their decision-making.

In the Foucauldian sense, discipline is not simply about material power and coercion, but also about the shaping of categorical meanings: what it means to be a state, what development means, indeed even what individuals are (biopolitics). The extent to which sovereignty, progress and personhood are articulated through liberal market metaphors – what Mick Moore calls 'implicit market surrogates' (1989: 1734) – or indeed *directly* as components of a market is the extent to which the disciplinary impetus of neoliberalism flows through global politics, producing power and authority even in the absence of explicitly punitive/coercive mechanisms. Accompanying the discursive power of depoliticisation is the claim that neoliberalism is 'common sense' – even to the degree that aspects of it might become constitutionalised (Glinavos 2008: 1089). As neoliberalism has established itself in policymaking and development thinking, those who advocate it have claimed that the constituent parts of a neoliberal platform are universally agreed upon (Hay 2004: 502).

Neoliberalism and class

For some, neoliberalism's discursive power is an expression of the politics of changing class relations, notably the undermining of labour and social democracy in favour of capital, and especially international and Western capital. This retrogressive 'class victory' emerged out of a period of falling profitability that ran through most Western economies throughout the 1970s and that led governments to implement policies that undermined organised labour and liberalised and subsidised financial capital in its search for enhanced profitability (Dumènil and Lèvy 2001; Overbeek and van der Pijl 1993). Within this perspective, neoliberalism is associated with a repression of wages, the creation of financial 'bubbles', rising public debt, complex 'financial instruments' (which are private speculatively created forms of debt) and an increasing social differentiation (Kotz 2008; Wolfson 2003).

Within this perspective, state action to forge a new class disposition is crucial (Harvey 2007), and neoliberalism is seen as a class project rather than an ideologically driven project, leaving open the possibility that neoliberalism might be imposed on some and not others – in the South as well as the North (Petras et al. 2006; Patel and McMichael 2004). It also allows us to understand neoliberalism as a 'strategy' or ideology of capital which might become part of class struggles in any part of the world, not necessarily according to any global division between North and South (Harman 2008). If the *raison d'être* of neoliberalism is to assist capital in its ongoing necessity to engage with workers and to extract surplus from them, it becomes only as good as its ability to improve the politics of capitalist hegemony. As such, it is a capitalist ideology, but hardly the *only* capitalist ideology.

Neoliberalism as practice

Neoliberalism is not a disembodied, aspatial, pre-formed external unity but involves actually existing people engaged in situated, grounded practices and governmental technologies that produce particular places and particular outcomes in those places. (England and Ward 2002: 250)

We have seen how, from the early 1980s, there have emerged a series of ideas and policies to remove the state from the economy, to promote economic liberalisation, and to 'see' societies as constituted by acquisitive/instrumental rational individuals. These developments have led critical scholars to portray these changes as an integrated project called neoliberalism which is driven by a set of interrelated agendas: to homogenise socio-cultural diversity, to project Western power throughout the world, to construct a global market order and to reconfigure class relations in favour of property.

We do not need to work through these critical points systematically in order to evaluate their relative merits and compatibility with each other. Their desire to challenge the free-market consensus from a progressive point of view is clear enough, and this book shares that view. What matters more specifically for our purposes is to get a clear sense of the meaning of neoliberalism in regard to Africa and the broad programme of social engineering it has undergone over the last thirty years. Recall that we are using the term 'neoliberalism' to encompass a diverse set of interventions in Africa over a protracted period which have as their orientation – to recall the three-point definition formed earlier – the removal of political control over the economy, the free market, and the rational individual.

Our understanding of neoliberalism will evoke aspects of the critiques listed above – some more than others. But what drives our use of neoliberalism as a concept is a need to *interpret practice*. This book will outline its approach to social practice fully in Chapter 3 with reference to pragmatist social theory. The rest of this chapter will outline the importance of this approach in regard to our understanding of neoliberalism as global social engineering and in light of the different critical definitions sketched above. The concern that drives discussion below is that any understanding of neoliberalism as a 'global project', executed over decades, runs a real risk of becoming deterministic in its politics and neglectful of agency in its analysis. One of the core narratives of this book is an insistence on the value of approaching neoliberalism as a global project, but this does not render impossible a recognition of agency, complexity and indeterminacy.

Interpretation is not description, and it is not a science. It requires normative and associative effort. The former simply means that we make judgements concerning the nature of the focus of our interest. The latter means that we endeavour to connect (or associate) discrete phenomena and to make some representation of these connections as a whole entity. Richard Peet offers a useful term of reference for neoliberalism: of a 'composite rather than a unity' (2002: 59); that is, to identify connections but not to strive to portray neoliberalism as a perfectly integrated and coherent project. It means that we will look at a variety of development policies and practices, evaluate them and represent them as part of a single neoliberal project in the loosest sense but with an awareness that without these loose connections we lose the insights offered by critical understandings of neoliberalism. Of course, the danger here is that our interpretive licence allows us to represent *every* aspect of development as part of one grand neoliberal scheme. One can imagine that in this situation it would be easy to fall into tautological conspiracy theory: all development is neoliberal, therefore neoliberals have planned it and all development outcomes serve 'neoliberal' purposes. This kind of circularity and caricature must be avoided because ultimately *'cui bono* [who benefits?] arguments ... rest on circumstantial evidence, rather than focussing on the agency of specific actors involved in implementing these [neoliberal] measures' (Knafo 2007: 191)

Another pitfall of some approaches to neoliberalism is that it tempts us to make an agent out of a concept – a 'universally inevitable monolithic force' in England and Ward's analysis (2002: 250), which bears some affinities with our approach here. In other words, once we have cast 'neoliberalism ... as an entity' acting upon Africa (Ong 2007a: 4), aspects of economic liberalisation can be attributed to neoliberalism *sui generis*. In some critical analysis, one might see phrases such as 'neoliberalism has sought to transform the constitution of persons' (Kingfisher and Maskovsky 2008), or neoliberalism as 'imbued with a Promethean impulse' (Heron 2008: 89). And advocates of neoliberalism also rely on the ideational fatalism that is contained by understanding economic concepts as actors in themselves: 'the market is telling you...' (World Bank advice to Government of Jamaica, cited in Weis 2004: 471). The difficulty here is that, although there is a kind of rough heuristic to this sort of statement, it is also the case that neoliberalism per se does nothing. And this produces a certain danger, which is well stated in a discussion of neoliberal globalisation: 'analyses ... are littered with sentences where globalisation "does" things. This reifies globalisation and draws an image of it as a force at work outside the reach of social actors' (Olesen 2005: 52). Rather, *people* act to promote politically and ideologically infused ends, and their actions and the premises that they are based in can be interpreted as part of a broader pattern of social action which one can label as neoliberalism. It is important to maintain that neoliberalism is nothing other than an interpretive endeavour to bring critical insight into more discrete practices pursued by particular agents. In itself, neoliberalism does nothing; its 'presence' emerges through its embodiment in discourse and practice, and only then through the effort of interpretation and critical reconstruction (we will look more closely at these matters in the next chapter).

Of course, at this point, there is a strong argument against our approach: by rejecting the notion that neoliberalism has causal efficacy and by claiming that neoliberalism is only 'present' in social practices, it appears that our understanding of neoliberalism is behaviouralist and voluntarist. To pose the challenge to our approach as a question: if neoliberalism is so damaging, why doesn't everyone stop practising it? But, even if neoliberalism doesn't act in itself, it does act upon agents through the actions of others. Indeed, the main reason for using the term 'social practice' is to avoid any sense that agencies are unencumbered by social influences that might have properties resembling structures when these influences are very strong. The point is simply that these social influences are only identifiable through the observation and interpretation of practice – by looking not simply at individual actions but at 'bundles' of actions that might be termed practices. Otherwise, any awareness of external influence or 'structuration' has to be defined as external, *a priori*, or even metaphysical (how some have interpreted Adam Smith's notion of an invisible hand).

In sum, neoliberalism is an abstraction, but its value derives primarily from the way it enables us to interpret practice, rather than the grand statements it might enable us to make. But what do we mean by 'practice'? Is this an appeal to a simplistic empiricism in which we assume that we can account for actions as if they are straightforward 'facts'? There are long-standing theoretical debates about the status of facts and their relation to discourse which need not detain us here. What we can do is state openly the premiss that this book relies upon: concrete actions will always contain a 'fixed' and 'factual' element, but equally they will always contain a discursive or constructed element. In other words, although a plain act – say the kicking of a ball – is incontestable as a fact (it either happened or it didn't), it is impossible to declare this fact without some recourse to language, imagery and, more broadly, a range of normative and political paraphernalia. For example the statement 'he kicked the ball' immediately composes gendered values as well as evoking pre-existing and constructed notions about football. Put simply: fact and value are mutually constitutive. This short detour into the ontology of acts allows us to think politically about practice because it treats even the most mundane acts as social acts. Therefore, we need to look at practice interpretively rather than descriptively, and we are fortunate enough to have a very useful body of work to rely upon in this respect: pragmatism. We will look at this in more detail in Chapter 3, but it is worth making a sketch in this overview chapter as well.

Pragmatism here does not refer to the common understanding of making decisions based on what is most simple, easy or effective – 'whatever is best administered is best' – far less to the hackneyed references to pragmatism used in conservative arguments about the 'real world'. Rather, it derives from John Dewey's attempts to understand the prospects for liberal social reform in early-twentieth-century America (Campbell 1995: chs 4 and 5). Pragmatism posits the following core values:

- All practice is social. There are no natural or non-political practices.
- Each act is part of a bundle of practices (habits) that enable each other and constitute what might be understood as social projects.
- Practices can be evaluated not just by their effects (ends) but also in themselves as value-laden.

The value of this approach can be seen more clearly by recalling some of the points made earlier in this chapter. First, I have noted that one key criticism of neoliberalism has been that it depoliticises development, claiming that liberalisation is 'scientific' or 'common sense'. Pragmatism is based on the refutation of this: all practice is political, based in values and expectations about the meaning and effects of practice. In fact, one of Dewey's main points is that social projects based in positivist models are often problematic because of the scientific assumptions that they make about predictability, cause and effect, and knowledge (Dewey 1929). The core of any attempt to 'repoliticise' the ostensibly value-neutral claims of market reformers is to think of neoliberalism as social practice.

Second, I have suggested that some critical approaches have represented neoliberalism as a grand/global project at the expense of agency and complexity, perhaps even lending neoliberalism agency in itself. I argued that it was necessary to focus on agency and complexity, but not simply to discard the merits of a critical and abstract concept like neoliberalism. Here, the interpretive bundling together of specific practices offers us a clearly formulated way forward: to make revealing associations between different aspects of neoliberal reform as practice requires that we necessarily maintain throughout a focus on social practices in order to develop meaningful abstractions.

Third, the assigning of neoliberalism as agency and the confusion of means and ends embedded in conspiracy narratives are resolved by understanding all practices as means *and ends* in themselves. Any purported prospective outcome is not a scientific deduction but a discursive component of a more specific observable act and in that sense a political act in itself – very often a way of justifying a practice that has harmful direct and immediate repercussions. At best, the 'ends' of a development programme or policy are a final act in a series.

Neoliberalism's boundaries

As we have seen, neoliberalism can mean different things to different people: ideology, discourse, form of political discipline, economic doctrine or class project. Each of these understandings has built within it a sense of the scope of action of neoliberalism. For example, as an economic doctrine, neoliberalism works within the economy to forge 'free' markets through reforms such as privatisation or the removal of subsidies. As a discourse, it aims to change the way (certain) people think about development by providing a different 'grammar' concerning social change and economic management. As a class project, neoliberalism works on the state and the economy to realign a balance of power between a capitalist class and the working classes. The general point here is that, although all critical commentary starts with a view of neoliberalism as 'economic' in its core (economic liberalisation), its prefix 'neo' seems to suggest that its zone of action goes beyond the economy that was the province of orthodox economics.

It is a core argument of this book that neoliberalism is best understood as social engineering. That is, neoliberalism as practice affects not only the economic sphere but also the state, the state's relations with society, and society itself. The image of a neoliberal *economics* is in fact an ideological one, claiming as it does that neoliberal reforms are solely concerned with economic efficiency, and 'getting the prices right' for a free market, and that it does not involve itself (unless absolutely necessary) in the more 'contentious' areas of governance or social relations. To the contrary, neoliberalism encapsulates a bundle of practices which pervade all aspects of political economy.

The notion of an economy (as classical political economists such as Adam Smith in fact recognised very well) can only make sense in the context of certain understandings of state power and also the norms and values of societies (Turner 2008). There is no aspect of neoliberalism that is not at once an intervention in the economy, polity and society.

Let us take a core and highly economistic aspect of neoliberalism – currency devaluation – to illustrate. Hard-wired into all IMF packages in the 1980s, currency devaluation became a *sine qua non* of structural adjustment throughout Africa. Countries embarking on structural adjustment experienced sometimes drastic currency depreciation as a result. The argument was that this would make exports more competitive and allow prices to reflect the 'real' value and scarcity of imports. But exchange rate liberalisation required the political will of the elite within the executive of the state – an elite that had often benefited from controlled exchange rates by virtue of its access to dollars, connections to central banks and controlled import markets. The essence of this is that overvalued currencies allowed elites with access to foreign exchange to import luxury goods extremely cheaply. As a result, devaluation was not 'apolitical' because it had to address substantial social resistance and in some instances had to be enforced through threats by the World Bank and the IMF as well as resignations or reshuffles within governments (Tanzania and Zambia are perhaps the clearest examples here).

After devaluation, the sometimes drastic increase in the price of key imports – especially staple foods and oil – damaged the ability of poor urban residents to make ends meet, leading to social protest and rebellion: the so-called IMF riots of the 1980s (Riley and Parfitt 1994; Toussaint 2008: 215–21). This led governments to make political decisions concerning whether they should suppress social protest or attempt to mollify the reform commitments written into structural adjustment programmes (SAPs), a dilemma that Thandika Mkandawire calls negotiating with 'two constituencies' in 'choiceless democracies' (1999; see also Hanson and Hentz 1999), intermixing vernacular politics of legitimacy, claims to sovereignty and references to good policy science. Thus, neoliberalism reform was – *ab initio* and incrementally – a political project.

Neoliberal practice came to involve itself in the form of the state: its institutions, personnel and abilities. As social protest against neoliberalism persisted more or less forcefully in most countries, one aspect of neoliberal reform encapsulated the disciplining of populations (Duffield 2001). This might involve force, but it also involves attempts to legitimise reforms and further to shape parts of society in the image of neoliberalism (Abrahamsen 2000). To take the first aspect, neoliberal reforms were increasingly associated with liberal political practice: transparency, accountability, efficiency and participation (Harrison 2001). The collective noun for this bundle of practices is good government, or simply governance. It enabled a series of reforms which aimed to create legitimate political processes to accompany ongoing processes of marketisation.

In countries where governance reforms were perceived by officials and donors as relatively advanced, the possibility of a more proactive neoliberal social engineering became more prominent and possible, incorporating an ambition not only to reconfigure the state but also to imagine how a reconfigured state might reconfigure a national society. Neoliberalism as a social model is premissed on the notion of society as fundamentally constituted by rational individuals. Thus, states might implement policies to reinforce social identities associated with neoliberalism: the customer or client, the businessperson, the small farmer (not the collective and class-infused category of the peasantry) or the voter. And, in order to do this, states might attempt to extend the remit of neoliberal reforms through programmes of education, decentralisation and local government reform.

This brief account should give the reader a sense of an expansive project which was – *ab initio* – political and economic but which has tended towards an increasingly explicit and sophisticated attempt at social engineering. In sum, the apparent economic kernel that is manifest in specific reforms such as devaluation also required both political and social management, a fact that has led neoliberalism as a bundle of practices to expand from the narrow negotiations between the IMF and a ministry of finance to a programme of social engineering which contains within it discursive, ideological and class-based facets. The history of neoliberalism in

Africa has been of an expanding frontier, of increasingly broad-based and ambitious practices to make African countries in the neoliberal image. The rest of this book will analyse this project and the practices that it has evoked and involved.

2

Neoliberalism in Africa:
a failed ideology

THIS CHAPTER provides an overview of the impact of neoliberal policies in Africa. It shows how they have failed to generate socio-economic recovery or development in Africa. The claims made by advocates of neoliberalism have constantly referred in some way or other to the prospective ability of a reduced role for the state and the dynamism of the competitive market to promote both economic growth and also a broader social well-being – even pro-poor growth. But, the evidence for these claims is slender at best. In order to substantiate this claim, one has to resort to a series of abstract statistical performances and/or claim that neoliberal policies were/are still embryonic in their implementation and effects, and therefore we are only witnessing the 'green shoots' of recovery – a recovery which is, however meagre, better than any realistic counterfactuals. Both of these developmental narratives concerning the impact of neoliberal policies seem rather unconvincing: after all, many states have been undergoing neoliberal reform for over twenty years. Neoliberalism has become the development doctrine of a generation in Africa; although a cautious optimism might have been sustainable five years into reform (on the grounds that there were signs of development), it is difficult to see how neoliberalism can be defended as a development programme after twenty years when the evidence points to nothing more than a scattering of moderate increases in gross national income (GNI) from the mid-1990s to the early 2000s which might be used in a series of regressions to show how things could be worse and how things might get better.

The chapter goes on to consider how neoliberalism has persisted in the face of such weak evidence of development recovery. It emphasises the institutional impetus behind neoliberal policies and how the practices embedded in these institutions have created a certain degree of immanence in neoliberal problem-solving. In other words, development practice has come to couch its problems and solutions in neoliberal terms. The chapter also looks at the ways in which the implementation of basic neoliberal policy doctrines has generated a particular kind of unstable political liberalisation.

It is easy to apprehend the broad contours of development failure: African economies have either been in decline, stagnant, or grown relatively slowly over the last generation. At a more concrete level, one can see the ways in which the economic decline is reflected in people's livelihoods. Working lives have become more intense, less secure, and more likely to involve multiple forms of work, none of which adequately secures a living (Ellis 2000; Bryceson et al. 2000; Gibbon et al. 1993, Woodehouse 2003). It is remarkable, then, that throughout the last generation (say, twenty-five years, which staggeringly for some countries is not that far off the average life expectancy) we have witnessed the rise *and rise* of a well-integrated and increasingly ambitious neoliberal development ideology.

It is now commonly (and rightly) understood that post-colonial nationalist/socialist development projects failed in sub-Saharan Africa. There are many different normative positions regarding the intrinsic merits of nationalist/socialist frameworks in Africa, but most historiographies recognise that a key symptom of the failure of these projects was a palpable economic slowdown and in some cases crisis that commenced in the early 1970s and came to a head by the end of the 1980s (Saul 2005; Sandbrook 1985). Simplistically – but representatively – one might say that a model was tried, suffered from various shortcomings, led to severe economic underperformance and thus was abandoned. In light of this, it is all the more remarkable that the subsequent development project – neoliberalism – was tried, suffered from various shortcomings that generated *even worse* economic performance but continued to be implemented in an increasingly virile and encompassing fashion. It is this apparent paradox that drives this chapter. Who can reasonably say that, after twenty-five years, neoliberalism has succeeded in promoting development in Africa?

Mapping neoliberal failure

Neoliberalism codified: structural adjustment

> The reform programmes that many African countries initiated in the mid-1980s – with the support of the IMF and World Bank and other donors – reflected a new paradigm. The reforms attempted to reduce the state's role in production and in regulating economic activity ... they placed more emphasis on maintaining macroeconomic stability and avoiding overvalued exchange rates ... this new paradigm became known as structural adjustment. (World Bank 1994a: 34)

As argued in the previous chapter, neoliberalism doesn't act; rather, it is a way of interpreting acts and policies. For Africa – in keeping with the other debt-distressed post-colonial and post-communist regions – neoliberal ideas were translated into a raft of macroeconomic policies, generally known as structural adjustment.

Neoliberalism came to Africa from outside. It was not an indigenously conceived project by any stretch of the imagination. Rather, starting in Senegal in 1979 (van de Walle 2001: 215), structural adjustment programmes set out an economic liberalisation agenda, attached to regular reform audit and the disbursement or rescheduling of credit. By the end of the 1980s, thirty-six African states had undergone 243 separate adjustment agreements with the World Bank and IMF (Chazan et al. 1999: 337); and by the end of the 1990s at least twenty-nine countries had suffered about a decade of structural adjustment (Hanson and Hentz 1999: 479), made up of various agreements. Thus it is fair to say that from the early 1980s, Africa was subjected to a pervasive and concerted project of economic liberalisation: a project that was aggressively advocated, funded and monitored by the World Bank and the IMF. Structural adjustment became, in effect, the development orthodoxy for the continent.

The structural adjustment programme (SAP) is best understood as a template. Although it is correct that not all SAPs were the same, country-specific policies attached themselves to a 'routine' programme of economic liberalisation. The core policies within SAPs were: the removal of exchange rate controls and consequent likely devaluation, the reduction of money supply and relatedly reduced public expenditure, increased rates of interest, the removal of price controls and public marketing institutions, and some kind of plan to open the economy more fully to FDI and relatedly privatisation (Simon et al. 2005, Harvey 1991: 121).

During the 1980s, average incomes in sub-Saharan Africa had fallen by about 20 per cent (Marquette 2003: 35), leaving the average African poorer than she was in 1970 (World Bank 2000: 14) or the early 1960s (World Bank 2000: 1, Mkandawire 2004b: 301). Between 1982 and 1995, the continent as a whole experienced only three years of (meagre) positive growth (Mkandawire 2004b: 321); over a broadly similar period, average GDP in Africa grew by less than 1 per cent leaving over 50 per cent of the population on less than a dollar a day (Sahn, Dorosh, and Younger 1997: 1, 24). Between 1981 and 2001, the number of poor people (people below the international poverty line) *doubled*, reaching 313 million (Round 2007, Table 3). It is also the case that SAP had a swingeing effect on general basic social entitlements – effects that are not ameliorated through some moderate palliatives of PRSP (SAPRIN 2004).

During the period from the early 1980s to the late 1990s, levels of external debt increased dramatically (Clapham 1996: 166–7; Chazan et al. 1999: 325–6). Increasing levels of debt have persisted up until very recently, standing at US$185 billion in 2003 (Commission for Africa 2005: 55). Since then, bilateral debt write-offs have reduced nominal international debt, but it remains to be seen how much of an impact the initiatives by the G8, the World Bank and the IMF in the new millennium will have on debt levels, although the extent to which HIPC and bilateral debt write-off will have an impact is certainly contested (Bond 2005: 221, Hanlon 2006: 212, Toussaint 2008: 186). Throughout this twenty-five-year period (the 'neoliberal generation'?), most countries have paid out massive amounts of money in interest, which throws into some doubt standard aid narratives that the West routinely gives to Africa (Hanlon 2000: 877; Pettifor and Garret 2000; Prempeh 2006).

In sum, structural adjustment did not deal with economic stagnation or high levels of external debt in Africa. Nor was there a robust investment response by international capital (Callaghy 1996). In fact, the liberalisation of financial regulation in many states served to exacerbate capital flight from Africa by those wealthy and mobile enough to pursue this policy (Mkandawire 2004a: 325), although remittances into the continent from African diasporas is also very significant. The bulk of foreign direct investment (FDI) in Africa has been focused in mining/extraction, especially oil (Klare and Volman 2006), which has proven to be either minimally beneficial or socially deleterious to Africans' well-being (Ferguson 2006: 198ff.; cf. Ross 1999; Bush 2004). In terms of health, Africa is currently in an extremely dire condition. An estimated 29.4 million people in sub-Saharan Africa have HIV/AIDS (UNAIDS/WHO 2003); malaria remains at epidemic levels as the campaigns against the anopheles mosquito have been abandoned and the virus adapts to existing prophylactics, killing up to a million people a year; and 300 million Africans remain without access to safe water, which is the basic prerequisite for a minimally healthy life (Commission for Africa 2005: 41). Neoliberal policies have signally failed to deal with the mass public health and mortality crisis produced by the prevalence of HIV/AIDS (Poku and Whiteside 2004; O'Manique 2004), and in Jean Comaroff's view AIDS and neoliberal sovereignties in Africa are co-constitutive of an international order in which Africa is actively excluded in the sense developed originally by Agamben (Comaroff 2006; see also Agamben 2005).

The social impact of economic liberalisation has been severe, although one should bear in mind that many social services provided by states had all but broken down in the period running up to structural adjustment. Poor rates of economic growth combined with a reduction in state expenditure on health and education to exacerbate social hardship (Adepoju 1993; Cornia et al. 1987; Onimode 1989). Some countries introduced user fees, which reduced levels of access to basic health and education.

Neoliberalism recodified: HIPC and PRSP

This dour record – and the social resistance and instability that it has provoked (Harrison 2002; Amenga-Etego and Grusky 2005) – put considerable pressure on those driving SAPs onwards (throughout the 1980s, these people were largely sited within the World Bank and the IMF) to modify the nature of the neoliberal policies 'codified' within SAPs. In the words of the World Bank, 'market driven development could not succeed without a strong social and institutional infrastructure, including a strong state' (World Bank 2000a: 38). As a result, from the late 1980s, transitory social amelioration packages were attached to core neoliberal reforms. Subsequently, a series of ad hoc debt reduction and rescheduling packages were implemented, leading to the more concerted Highly Indebted Poor Countries (HIPC) scheme, inaugurated in 1996 and 'enhanced' in 1999. The HIPC scheme was premised on demonstrable commitment (if not progress) under SAP (minimum of three years' satisfactory adherence to an IMF structural reform programme), with the incentive to attain a debt write-down to a 'sustainable' level of debt, which was expected to release money for a renewed effort at social expenditure, especially in primary health care and education.

Also in 1999 – and matching HIPC debt relief with a new funding/credit framework – SAP was replaced by the Poverty Reduction Strategy Paper (PRSP) and its related funding mechanisms within the World Bank and the IMF (the Poverty Reduction Strategy Credit and the Poverty Reduction and Growth Facility respectively). The PRSP is a 'post-Washington Consensus' development template (Fine et al. 2001): it has a greater emphasis on social expenditure, less *explicit* talk of policy conditionality (but see World Bank 2005), and an emphasis on borrowing government ownership rather than World Bank and IMF intervention. We will go on to look at PRSPs in more detail in later chapters. The point here is not to claim that HIPC or PRSPs are structural adjustment in disguise – although in a bare empirical sense they maintain both the macroeconomic liberalism of SAP and (contrary to some World Bank and IMF spin) they do maintain policy conditionalities. But, analytically, this tends to evoke the kinds of conspiratorial approach rejected in the previous chapter that saw changes in institutions and practices as motivated by an overarching interest or abstract source of power (ideational or material). Instead, in this chapter, we understand innovations such as HIPC and PRSP as changes in neoliberal policy, as iterated attempts to recodify the neoliberal world-view of market, state and self into different procedures and institutions. This is a significant process, not window dressing. As we shall see in subsequent chapters, it has enabled the expansion of neoliberal social practice and facilitated increasingly ambitious discourses of social engineering – away from macroeconomic recalibrating 'shocks' (for example a shift to the rudimentaries of cash budgeting) and towards deeper social transitions. The material basis for the construction of the governance architecture is the Highly Indebted Poor Countries scheme, agreed in 1996 and revised as Enhanced HIPC in 1999. Being accepted as a HIPC country enables a country to receive a write-off of outstanding debt and capital stock to what international finance organisations judge a 'sustainable' level. A sustainable level is a debt-to-export ratio of 150 per cent. Gaining HIPC status revolves around donor evaluations of an indebted country, and these evaluations are based on the level of indebtedness, indicators of poverty, and the track record of a country in implementing structural adjustment programmes. These evaluations are led by the World Bank and the IMF, and in fact the key criterion for accession to HIPC is a country's previous performance in Bank and Fund adjustment policies. Furthermore, HIPC status is only given to countries that borrow exclusively from the Bank's 'soft' lending body, the International Development Association (IDA). Uganda, Tanzania and Mozambique – Africa's first three countries to gain HIPC status – have been through a broadly similar process: each has introduced structural adjustment, weathered the social and political turbulence that this has created, and subsequently managed to 'lock in' neoliberal fundamentals, mainly associated with the IMF's macroeconomic concerns with budget deficits and rates of inflation. Bank and IMF boards determine a country's eligibility for HIPC – known as decision point; further reforms are then set out in further documentation (described below), leading to completion point, when the Bank and bilateral donors (members of the 'Paris Club' of creditors) disburse all concessional debt reduction. The completion point is supposed to mark a country's liberation from unsustainable debt; it is a once-and-for-all moment.

Thus HIPC represents a selective engagement by the Bank and the IMF in Africa, although a fairly restrictive list of HIPC states is expanding (thirteen states in 2003). HIPC is premissed on a 'secure' macroeconomic environment that makes the outright freezing of programme lending unlikely. But HIPC is also the starting point for a new raft of lending programmes (which might make heavily indebted countries *more* indebted in the medium term). The World Bank manages an expansive lending portfolio, detailed in its Country Assistance Strategy (CAS) documents. The CAS outlines the Bank's lending in various sectors of public action – all integrated into a detailed matrix. There are two noteworthy aspects of the CAS in terms of the nature of the politics of external intervention.

First, Bank lending is often formulated as a sector investment programme (SIP). Broadly consonant with sector-wide approaches (SWAps) which many bilateral donors now adopt to some extent, the Bank lends money to a specific sector – say, education or roads – without making any specific project intervention with specific conditionalities. The idea behind this is that it allows government ministries to take 'ownership' of reform: a ministry provides a detailed programme of projects and donors/creditors (perhaps collectively through 'basket funds') and makes substantial financial contributions to the sector-wide plan.

But the second point is that the CAS strongly revises the extent to which governments can be said to own their sectoral plan. Donors continue to monitor very closely sectoral development. In fact there is often more surveillance of public action than before. The Bank's CAS contains mechanisms of 'displaced conditionality': specific project demands made as conditions for the release of funds are played down, whilst performance indicators are emphasised, triggers for the release of money detailed, and benchmarks established. The CAS also bases its funding projections on 'high' and 'low' cases: if a government implements reforms speedily and efficiently, it receives more money more quickly; if it fails to implement reforms according to performance indicators and the targets they establish, a government might lose substantial amounts of concessional lending. Collectively, mechanisms such as these hardly betray a loosening of external control over reform; there is, rather, a stronger sense of local custodianship.

The CAS provides a schedule of the creation of the PRSP. This is the key government document within the architecture of governance. The PRSP defines, in substantial detail, a raft of programmatic reforms and projects to implement a pro-poor development strategy. PRSPs key into the Millennium Development Goals and often make ambitious claims concerning the improvement of social well-being. It is supposed to be country-driven, results-oriented (rather than based on indicative spending targets), and deal with public action in all its aspects. The PRSP is based on previous comprehensive development frameworks (CDFs) and, like CDFs, the PRSP aims to establish a 'shop window' for donors: to demonstrate a concerted and well-thought-through strategy to combat poverty. Countries might produce an interim PRSP or a full PRSP, the former allowing limited debt relief (write-off of interest but not debt stock).

A PRSP is the prerequisite for HIPC status. Some PRSPs have been based on previously existing programmes and some are entirely new. They involve detailed plans to develop new monitoring and surveillance techniques, new forms of statistical processing, new forms of budgetary management, logical frameworks of spending and output scheduling, and a long and detailed 'matrix' of execution. The Bank has produced a *PRSP Sourcebook* to 'assist' countries in developing PRSPs. Each PRSP is then evaluated by a Joint Staff Assessment (JSA), held by the World Bank and IMF. Only JSA approval will lead to HIPC status, debt write-off and access to new waves of external credit and loan. The HIPC decision point is given, after which (either by 'fast' or 'slow' track) a HIPC country is closely monitored and awarded completion point.

PRSPs are financed by the World Bank through poverty reduction support credits (PRSCs) and by the IMF through poverty reduction and growth facilities (PRGFs). The PRSC funding schedule is oriented towards the CAS; the credit is on 'IDA' terms; it is multi-sectoral; and it is focused on 'pro-poor' reforms. The aim is to synchronise both the PRSP and the CAS around the PRSC, and to present the PRSC as a single programme to coordinate other donor lending.

And yet, for all these shifts in neoliberal codification, no great developmental shift has happened or seems even *likely* to happen. No analogy with the abandonment of national statist developmentalism which took place in the late 1970s has occurred, even though the neoliberal model has performed so poorly by any developmental criteria. Why?

African states in a neoliberal age

There was a time when the answer to this las question would seem very straightforward. Throughout the 1980s, African states were subjected to pervasive compulsion by the international finance institutions (IFIs): the World Bank and the IMF. Governments on the verge of insolvency would engage with the IFIs in order to gain further credit and debt rescheduling; in return the IFIs would set out a series of economic conditionalities which governments would have to implement. In the first place, these conditionalities were similar for all states and were informed by neoliberal macroeconomics (Simon et al. 1995: 4; Campbell and Loxley 1989; Ghai 1991): devalue/liberalise the currency, reduce public expenditure, remove public control of interest rates, and abolish price and marketing controls. These reforms created economic turbulence and recession; they also imposed economic hardship on large sections of the population. Thus, states often had to impose these policies against social protest and rebellion (Riley and Parfitt 1994; Harrison 2002: ch. 3; Lugalla 1995; Mkandawire and Olukoshi 1995).

As a result of the tensions outlined above, the 1980s were characterised by a familiar set of scenes, played out in different sequences on different national stages: governments agree a structural adjustment package based on neoliberal conditionalities, some aspects of the SAP are implemented, social protest emerges in response to the effects of adjustment, smaller elite groups attempt to undermine aspects of the adjustment package, governments attack the IFIs for violating their sovereignty, governments attempt to renegotiate their SAP, the IFIs warn governments that they might be declared 'off track' or that further tranches of credit might be suspended, new agreements are brokered. This is why we have the striking statistic that during the 1980s, just thirty-six African states implemented 241 adjustment programmes (Owusu 2003: 1659): it is a testament to the halting, coercive and turbulent way in which neoliberalism was enforced by the IFIs in sub-Saharan Africa. Thus, the answer to the question that ended the last section might well be: neoliberalism remained the only development agenda throughout the 1980s because it was championed by powerful external agencies that compelled African states to pursue this agenda. An important contextual factor during this period was the end of the Cold War, which left African governments with no obvious alternative source of financial or political support outside of Western neoliberalism.

We will come to look at the social practices that constituted this adversarial neoliberal project in Chapter 4. What matters here are the repercussions of the sustained implementation of a failing development project. Any turbulence, protest or economic crisis that the neoliberal agenda provoked was the business of individual states, not the IFIs. As already noted in Chapter 1, Mkandawire (1999) coins the phrase 'two constituencies' for this reason: governments are (in some sense) accountable to their populations who are subjected to neoliberal reform, but they are also accountable to the IFIs who audit reform progress and make decisions as to whether progress has been sufficiently adequate to allow further releases of credit. Mkandawire's dichotomy is especially intriguing because whilst one 'constituency' (the IFIs) remained steadfastly undemocratic (in terms of accountability for their actions), the other 'constituency' was ostensibly being given universal franchise.

Between 1990 and 2004, multiparty elections were held in forty-two African countries (Rakner and Svasand 2005: 85). There was also a wave of constitutional revision which enshrined rights of expression and association. In some landmark examples, entrenched military or single-party presidents were replaced by new parties and presidents (e.g. Zambia, Benin, Malawi, Chad). And, of course, in 1994, South Africa experienced – with a high degree of peace, all things considered – its liberation elections. This 'second winds of change' or 'second liberation' in sub-Saharan Africa was underpinned by the establishing of 'democratic conditionalities' by major bilateral donors.

One might imagine that these changes – commonly referred to as 'democratisation' – might profoundly affect the conditionality politics of the IFIs and their relations with African states. Most obviously: if structural adjustment creates so much social hardship, wouldn't African voters replace 'neoliberal' ruling parties with parties that boasted alternative development strategies?

Multiparty elections have not tipped the balance between the 'two constituencies' in favour of an alternative to neoliberalism. Throughout the 1990s, structural adjustment remained the core development agenda of almost all African states, and those that seemed most unorthodox were hardly exemplars of a new popular democracy. In fact, a closer look at the *political practices* that have been associated with 'democratisation' in Africa reveals to us that multiparty constitutional states have become the template for African states implementing structural adjustment. Formal multipartyism and neoliberalism have coexisted reasonably easily, intermixed with other practices which, by and large, advocates of neoliberalism prefer not to emphasise. Let us elaborate the key practices.

In many countries, democratisation has often been effectively managed by incumbent elites. Former single-party presidents can reinvent themselves as 'democrats' (Baker 1998; Takougang 2003). Existing ruling parties can mobilise the resources of the state to marginalise opposition parties and sweeten key electoral constituencies (Rakner and Svasand 2005), whether through the distribution of electoral largesse, the seconding of public cars and buildings, or a bias in public radio broadcasts. Elections can be organised in ways that provide advantage to the incumbent, for example through the setting of constituency boundaries, interference in electoral commissions' organisation of voter lists, or plain electoral fraud such as ballot-box stuffing.

Opposition parties have emerged, but their social bases and ideologies have hardly fitted any hopeful liberal desire for polyarchy, let alone more radical, popular or socialist agendas. Instead – and quite unsurprisingly – parties have been forged out of factions of marginalised elites or 'small transient coteries' (Rakner and Svasand 2002: 32) some of whom might previously have been in government. These elites have demonstrated above all a desire to attain political sway and access to public resources and this has sometimes allowed leading opposition leaders to fall out with each other, taking fragile party organisations with them; it has also led to a fair amount of 'floor crossing' in which opposition leaders reconcile themselves to the incumbent party, often after securing access to a political portfolio (Rakner and Svasand 2002; Konings 2004). And, additionally, opposition party programmes and manifestos have, by and large, adhered to the neoliberal fundamentals that ruling parties are committed to. Most commonly, opposition parties promise a less corrupt version of the same neoliberal programme (May and Massey 2002: 82). And in many cases where opposition parties have been voted into office they have reconstructed many aspects of the centralising and presidential form of governance of their predecessors, as well as sticking just as closely to a neoliberal development script (e.g. Zambia, Malawi).

Bilateral donors have tempered any desire for democratisation with their own political concerns. Western states have generally put economic and geopolitical interests first. And, with regard to the form and content of governance, the ability of incumbent regimes to implement economic liberalisation and maintain 'order' takes precedence over the quality or even existence of multipartyism, let alone broader considerations of popular empowerment or social well-being. The case of Uganda reveals these tensions well (Reno 2002; Hearn 1999).

Thus, the West's record on tying aid to democratisation is actually rather poor (Brown 2005; Rye Olsen 1998; Crawford 1997) – in Crawford's phrase, 'high on rhetoric, low on delivery' (Crawford 2005: 572). In cases such as Burkina Faso, Ethiopia and Uganda, where civic rights and even party opposition have been denied for extended periods, Western states are happy to smooth over difficult political issues regarding democracy in order to support regimes that have been able to boast a concerted attempt at neoliberal reform (Brown 2005; Konings 2004: 303–4). Another symptom of the West's weak attachment to democratisation is the bland and evasive nature of Western electoral observer missions. The supposedly robust 'free and fair' criterion has been watered down to 'reasonably free and fair' or even 'reflects the general will of the electorate'. And, because the World Bank and the IMF wish to maintain an apolitical self-representation, both of these institutions have explicitly declared that they are not concerned about democratisation.

So far, we have established that the ostensible 'democratisation' process has been beset by the power of incumbency, the acquisitive nature of opposition parties, and the lukewarm commitment to democratisation by Western states. The outcome of this disposition is that democratisation has been largely 'performative'; that is, the shift towards multipartyism has been orchestrated in a way that allows for substantial continuity in the management of neoliberal reform and minimises the substance of enfranchisement for African populations. Through a different lens, it reveals how neoliberal practices have conflated multiparty politics and a range of political strategies pursued by competing elite factions. Formally democratic, committed to neoliberal development, supported by alignments of bilateral and multilateral Western agencies, this is how one can characterise the African neoliberal state in the present day.

Neoliberal politics

It gets worse. Beyond the weak and contingent commitments of many ruling elites to democratisation, it is also clear that the scope and nature of formal politics have been shaped in ways that restrict any putative democratic potential. This shaping has a great deal to do with the consolidation of neoliberalism in sub-Saharan Africa. Let us begin with a sketch.

In the first place, we should pay attention to the boundaries of legitimate political contest. It is clear that, from the 1990s onwards, the IFIs and other Western agencies have promoted the 'ring-fencing' of some aspects of public action away from public deliberation. There are a number of trends that collude in the doing of this. First, there is the rise of a strongly technical policy discourse, in which decisions regarding resource allocation or economic regulation are expressed in an economistic and 'scientific' language which appears to be value-neutral (Abrahamsen 2000) and therefore less amenable to normative or ideological contestation. This is what Ferguson is referring to in his evocative phrase 'scientific capitalism' (Ferguson 1995).

Second, neoliberal political analysis maintains a highly restrictive cordoning around what is understood as legitimate political advocacy. Rational-choice political economy, rent-seeking models, and a belief that a 'core' economic doctrine should be saved from any political intervention have led institutions such as the World Bank to worry about political parties and anti-neoliberal civic associations pursuing their 'vested interests' and creating the danger that the state might become 'captured' or 'biased' (Beckman 1993). Whilst it might be the case that better-resourced groups can lobby states to pursue factional and short-term interests, neoliberals have no clear way to judge between this tendency and the mere exercise of political pressure upon the state, which is, after all, at the heart of modern theories of liberal democracy such as those of Robert Dahl and Almond and Verba. Furthermore, by maintaining that there should be an apolitical economic orthodoxy at the heart of every state (the Consensus that lies behind both the Washington and post-Washington approaches), it is easy to render any political action that pulls this orthodoxy into question as somehow parochial or self-serving.

The framing of legitimate and illegitimate political practice is pernicious. It enables a celebration of civil society and political openness based on a neoliberal consensus (Kasfir 1998; Kamat 2004): that is, an acceptance of heavy external development interventions, a cleaving to structural adjustment and its epigones, and an acceptance of various discourses that have emerged within evolving neoliberal practice – social capital, transparency, participation and pro-poor growth, inter alia. This kind of 'neoliberal civil society' has indeed been to some extent constructed by donors through funding, agenda shaping, and an integration of NGOs into consultancy and service delivery mechanisms which involve little beyond neoliberal problem-solving (Mercer 2003; Hearn 2007).

Third, and related to both of the above, African states have become increasingly *habituated* in their dealings with the IFIs. In some cases, governments might have been managing aid and adjustment regimes for twenty years. It is unsurprising, then, that a highly integrated political milieu has emerged in which key civil servants, technicians and ministers have established areas of political management with in-country aid donors and World Bank/IMF 'missions' (Green 2003; Gould 2005). This 'realm of governance' (see Chapter 6) is identifiable in a series of political practices, clustered around regular meetings with donors and creditors, workshops, audit and policy management processes, and donor-funded 'technical assistance' (see Chapter 5). It constitutes an aspect of government which is substantially removed from whatever 'popular' politics and party politics might exist outside this 'realm'. *In extremis*, programmes are agreed in donor consultative groups before they go to parliament (Mozambique, Ghana); government documents are drafted, edited or authored by expatriate technical assistants (Tanzania, Ghana, Uganda); and a massive amount of information traffics between state and donors without the knowledge of any other institution within the country.

In short, the scope of political debate and contestation has been profoundly shaped by neoliberal designs of what constitutes 'the political' (Ayers 2006). And – however authoritarian pre-existing regimes might have been – it is fair to say that the ambit of legitimate and open democratic contestation in African states has been narrowly defined by neoliberal discourse and practice.

Governance

This brings us to another apparent paradox: more or less synchronously with the depoliticisation of 'democracy', donors and the IFIs have constructed an increasingly explicit political discourse for development policy thinking, known as governance, or good governance. From the early 1990s, emanating most strongly from the World Bank, development thinking has been guided by a series of interconnected political norms: transparency, participation, accountability, ownership, the rule of law and empowerment. These are all easily recognisable as part of the normative lexicon of political liberalism and, as such, they boast an affinity, or at least complementarity, with democratisation. In fact, in certain stances, these norms have left the Bank rather awkwardly denying that it is being 'political' or pro-democracy in employing these phrases in its policy documents (Marquette 2003). Thus, it would appear that the World Bank is both responsible for contributing to a narrowing and depoliticisation of the political sphere whilst also evoking a

more explicitly political language for its own development policy
lending.

The paradox is overcome by looking at reform practice. Understood within the context of the neoliberal project in Africa and our
recognition of it as expanding social practice, governance begins
to resemble an innovated repertoire of development management
tools. Governance is all about improving the efficacy of neoliberal
policy reform; in other words, it *contributes to* the anti-democratic
dispensation set out above. How so?

The governance lexicon listed above is not only mentioned in
grand public relations exercises such as the *World Development
Reports*; it is also drawn upon in policy documents. Public service
reform, financial management, decentralisation programmes, and
other aspects of governance reform are commonly funded by the
World Bank and related donors; in fact these kinds of reform would
simply be impossible without external funding, such is the extent
of African states' dependence on external finance. Two extreme
examples: Uganda relied on Official Development Assistance for 52
per cent of its annual budget in 2004 (Barkan and Kayunga et al.
2004); Ghana relied on aid flows for about 90 per cent of its public
investment expenditure during the 1990s (Williams 2008: 119).
The policy documents that accompany the funding programmes of
the World Bank and a range of Western bilateral donors commonly
speak of accountability, participation and so on, but rendered in
a specific fashion. These liberal desiderata are *instrumentalised*
as the means by which development policy might become more
effective. This is most evident in regard to the way 'participation'
has been integrated into aspects of World Bank policy. 'Participation' has largely been a tool for effective policy implementation,
a way to ensure that the subjects or targets of a policy comply
with its aims and objectives (Cooke and Kothari 2001; Mohan
and Stokke 2001). As a result, participation usually commences
after a project has been devised, and is organised in a way that
gives little room for the project to change. Furthermore, the term

'participation' has also been used to describe the introduction
of user fees, for example in water projects, which represents a
completely financialised understanding of the word.

Transparency has been employed as a normative drive to reform
financial, information and resource-management systems in ways
that make them more amenable to routine audit and expenditure
tracking, the latter being a key 'process conditionality' for general
budget support. Accountability has also been constructed within
neoliberal practice in contrast to broader political or more vernacular understandings of the term. Accountability is commonly
formulated to identify goods and service providers' relations with
clients or customers – a social vision constituted by utility-seeking
individuals: the service providers incentivised by wage increments
and output targets, the clients desiring 'value for money'.

These examples suggest that the liberal provenance of these
governance terms provides them with a compatibility with visions
of a neoliberal society. Indeed, it is clear that each of these terms
is articulated on the premiss that social interaction is based on
'rational' self-interested individuals who weigh up – through some
form of utilitarian mindset – the costs and benefits of alternative forms of action. This is why David Williams speaks of the
World Bank's governance agenda as based on an ontology of *Homo
oeconomicus* (1999), and it also accounts for Kamat's phrase 'the
entrepreneurial citizen', conflating ideas of political rights with a
disposition to liberal formulations of independence and autonomy
(2004: 164). The aggregation of this ontology of liberal individuals
is a society that tends towards equilibria as a result of positive-sum
socially beneficial interactions based on assumptions of Pareto
optimality (Vlachou and Christou 1999: 3; Cohen and Rogers
1992: 398).

This kind of neoliberal political vision is what Harrison (2001)
calls the 'anaesthetisation of politics' in which considerations of
social structure, conflict of interest and political struggle are
defined out of the frame of development politics. Ideologically, then,

contemporary formulations of participation, accountability and so on serve to construct a model of sociability in which resistance to neoliberal development policy seems far less thinkable. Although this point might seem rather abstract, one can see real effects of this approach to politics in the way that Poverty Reduction Strategy Papers – which are the central platform for development lending and policy in Africa – have been created (Gould 2005; Nyamagusira and Rowden 2002; Whitfield 2005). We will sketch this out below with particular attention to the implementation of modalities of ownership, but first a brief note on the PRSP, which – like governance and democratisation – integrates into neoliberalism's idealised perceptions of a market society.

Earlier in this chapter, we discussed the ways in which neoliberal interventions have been codified into different development policy templates. Starting with the externally dominated SAPs and progressing into more 'inclusive' (Craig and Porter 2005) PRSPs, the templates have tended to become more explicit about the fact that neoliberalism centrally involves changing political practices. Here, we look at the PRSPs more closely, as these are the current template for neoliberal development.

The PRSP framework was created by the World Bank and the IMF in 1999, and has emerged as the key requisite for the winning of HIPC status. It is a broad-ranging policy document that sets out key areas of prospective reform with a set of target expenditures and outcomes. PRSPs are heavily reliant on the governance lexicon for their normative framing and they are written on the understanding that they will shape the ways in which external donors might allocate resources to HIPC states. It is clear that PRSPs have allowed states to pay more attention, and allocate more resources, to social sectors. Unlike SAPs, poverty, health, education, HIV/AIDS and gender have been strongly foregrounded. It is also true that the expenditure matrices that are appended to PRSPs have set out increases in spending in these areas. In this sense, PRSPs certainly represent an improvement on the logic of

SAP, which was far more explicitly concerned with macroeconomic 'stabilisation'. Nevertheless, it is important to note that PRSPs are based on the premisses of SAP: they maintain an insistence on the neoliberal fundamentals of economic management and devise new ways of implementing aspects of that economic agenda more effectively; and they are premissed on the internalisation – especially through the Ministry of Finance – of strong and austere financial and budgetary management (Cammack 2002). What PRSPs have encapsulated, though, is a new set of political procedures that have rendered neoliberalism less of a stark external intervention than was previously the case during the 'adjustment decade' of the 1980s.

Perhaps the key term in the governance lexicon here is 'ownership'. Like participation, accountability and transparency (discussed above), this term has been formulated in a specific way and has had specific effects. 'Ownership' connotes a condition in which all agencies involved in a development policy perceive themselves as having a stake in it – which is why involved agencies are now commonly referred to as 'stakeholders' or 'partners' in development literature (relatedly, see Eade 2007). The key 'stakeholder' is the government, which should be in the 'driver's seat' in devising and implementing neoliberal development policy. PRSPs are ostensibly written by governments, not imposed by the IFIs, and they are supposed to reflect national priorities. But the substance of 'ownership' is very slight: because of the high levels of dependence on external funding, governments usually write PRSPs in ways that will meet the approval of the IFIs and therefore generate aid and credit through the IMF's Poverty Reduction and Growth Framework and the World Bank's Poverty Reduction Strategy Credit (relatedly, see Therkildsen 2000). In a nice turn of phrase, 'the shift to PRSP should not be exaggerated. Where before donors told governments what to do now governments largely tell donors what they want to hear' (*The Economist*, cited in Sumner 2006: 1407). Furthermore, the PRSP process is highly integrated into a set of procedures, set up under the Highly Indebted Poor Country framework, in which the World Bank and the IMF can ensure that PRSPs are compatible with their broader neoliberal world vision (see Chapter 2).

Thus it would seem that the extent of ownership – having been forged in the context of massive dependency on external funds – is limited by the IFIs' broader vision. Perhaps more appropriate terms than 'ownership' would be 'custodianship' or 'trusteeship' (Cowen and Shenton 1996; Whitfield 2005; Hewitt 2006)

Custodianship represents a significantly attenuated form of control. Ownership connotes a right of control, a kind of sovereignty in which decision-making arrogates to the owner – for our purposes a government. Quite simply, African states, infused with neoliberal practices that have a largely external provenance, do not own their development policy in any 'sovereign' sense. Rather, development policy is 'co-owned' by a raft of creditors and donors who fund substantial parts of almost all reforms, programmes and projects. And co-ownership does not necessarily mean parity: it might be that financially dependent states which host a welter of external agencies in their capital cities are largely practising the art of extraversion (Bayart 1993), a kind of alignment with powerful external forces for the purposes of assuring state stability and the reproduction of a ruling elite (see van de Walle 2001). In this sense, governments are not owners but custodians – reformulating state sovereignty away from decision-making to management control; charged with responsibilities of implementation, aiming to devise nationally specific versions of neoliberal templates, and perhaps innovating policy at the margins.

Thus, it is unsurprising that African governments involved in the PRSP process *have not* attempted to produce 'unorthodox' PRSPs (Sumner 2006: 1408). But this is not solely the result of the material power of external agencies. Ideally, for the IFIs, even in the absence of budgetary dependence on external finance and the ever-lurking possibility of sanctioning by the IMF or the

World Bank, governments would voluntarily adopt the neoliberal agenda of the PRSP, governance and so on (Abrahamsen 2004). Inasmuch as this has been successful in Africa so far, it has been the result of an effective *socialisation* of governing elites by the aid community as a whole. 'Governance' rather than 'adjustment' provides a far better politics to produce complicit elites in African governments, especially when a good chunk of governance lending is actually aimed at *reconstructing* states rather than rolling them back, for example in capacity building, public-service reform, decentralisation programmes and general budgetary support. It is through these reforms that neoliberalism has become increasingly 'embedded' within African states, producing transnational communities of neoliberal practice within their broader ambit, and based largely in the centres of capital cities, as we shall discuss more fully in Chapter 6.

In sum, governance has – in terms of both its discourse and its practice – served to socialise neoliberal policies into African states and societies: to make neoliberal reform more stable and less contested. It serves as a perfect counterpart to the narrowing 'democratic' space created by 'scientific capitalism' and aims to produce states which champion neoliberalism as much as the World Bank. In the next chapter, we will return to look again at pragmatism as a framework to understand social practice. This will give us the wherewithal to understand the socialisation of neoliberalism and its expanding remit in the subsequent three chapters: through the international, the national and the subnational.

Conclusion

Returning to the question that was posed in the first section – how has neoliberalism persisted throughout a protracted period of economic instability and decline? – we have an answer which is more complicated than merely a reference to the coercive capabilities of the IFIs, although this capability certainly remains part of the answer. What has evolved throughout the neoliberal generation is a more active shaping of political practice within African states. This has produced a certain kind of 'democracy' and a certain kind of 'governance', which are not only compatible with the forward drive of neoliberalism, but are *integrated components* of this drive. Neoliberalism is not an economic doctrine, it is a social doctrine – social engineering based on a certain understanding of the economy. Seen in this light, it is perfectly acceptable to imagine the forging of neoliberal states and societies which involve more complex policy platforms than merely removing a swathe of public regulation from the economy.

The neoliberal project remains largely an external contrivance. Its social base within African societies is restricted to governing elites that have adopted the post-conditionality mode of interaction with donors, and civil society organisations that have become part of the participation agenda and that are often dependent on external bilateral funding for their survival. One of the key reasons why the social base for neoliberalism is so narrow is the poor economic responses that neoliberal policy has evoked. Unless and until neoliberal reforms produce a reasonably stable and palpable improvement in general social well-being in African states, neoliberalism will remain an elite project, an external imposition, or an irrelevance to those excluded from the largesse of creditors and donors.

3

Practices of neoliberalism:
repertoires, habits and conduct

THE PREVIOUS two chapters have argued that neoliberalism is a core aspect of globalisation and that Africa's experience of neoliberalism informs us of key aspects of globalisation, just as European integration or Chinese late development might. We went on to consider how the concept of neoliberalism performs as a critical concept to understand Africa/globalisation. Here, we emphasised the importance of social practice above ideationally driven approaches or the teleologies that emerge by starting with *cui bono?* questions. We foreshadowed a pragmatist approach and suggested that this would allow us to understand neoliberalism as an expanding bundle of practices that might be understood as global social engineering. In the second chapter, we began to understand the strength of the neoliberal project by introducing it as the practice of development failure: not a confident and legitimate exercise but rather an embattled and combative project that has been underpinned by strong external intervention and the material fragility of African states. In this context, we mapped the contours of the practices that have shaped neoliberal governance.

In this chapter, we return to our theoretical framework. There is a need to take the kernel of pragmatism's theoretical features (as set out on pp. 30–31) and develop some more specific concepts that are dedicated to an analysis of neoliberal practice. This will provide us with an approach for the subsequent three chapters.

Sacred and profane neoliberalism

In Chapter 1 we introduced neoliberalism as based in three premisses concerning the self, the market and the state. These starting points underpin the various attempts to design and execute neoliberal policy, 'not to make a model that is more adequate to the real world, but to make the real world more adequate to its model' (Clarke 2005: 58). As such, the relationship between neoliberal ideas and social practice is utopian. That is, neoliberal social theory seems to be premissed on a faith that there is a competitive market society immanent (within the self-interestedness, utilitarianism and calculative rationality of humans) in all places which would serve everyone's best interests (through a combination of assumptions about positive-sum competition and Pareto social optimality). If this is the essential ontology of neoliberalism, then it is clearly based on a vision of human society that is unreal. It is unreal in the sense that it offers a vision of social relations that fails to capture the bulk of social interaction. Ideologies of states are negated and replaced by considerations of the science of efficiency (Ferguson 1995); moralities are atrophied into concerns with fairness within the market; forms of trust, gift-giving and reciprocity become social or human capital (Fine 1999); families become households; knowledge becomes education and skills (see Colclough 1996). In this sense, neoliberalism is sacred: it is derived as external to the social world and serves not only as a measure of various social realities but also as a way of speaking of – and evaluating – people, institutions, norms and so on.

Of course, there are many theoretical approaches to social relations that are highly selective and that set hard boundaries around what they consider to be relevant. What makes these points especially germane to neoliberalism, as we have already seen in Chapter 2, is simply that this world-view can be found within a great deal of policy thinking, political advocacy, international lending, credit and risk assessment, training/technical assistance, and intergovernmental economic regulation and law-making over the last thirty years; and it continues to be so. Thus neoliberalism is not simply unreal in the sense outlined above; it is *unrealised* – the (implicit or explicit) ideal-type of a neoliberal society is used to identify deviances and absences in actually existing societies by a range of powerful agencies and actors, which then endeavour to engineer proximate to the neoliberal model. These deviances and absences serve to enable real practices of intervention – it is in this sense that this book speaks of social engineering.

Here we come to a paradox. Neoliberalism's utopia can only be realised through agents who are themselves at most approximations or at least simulacra of the neoliberal self. And, of course, these agents necessarily engage in (or are part of) societies which are *not* neoliberal: this is the motivation for their interventions. If the *idea* of neoliberalism is ideal – pristine and self-contained in its vision of society and the self – the *practice* of neoliberalism is necessarily 'dirtier' (see Larner 2000; Ong 2007b). Neoliberal progress has proven to be complex, halting, contested and contradictory (Campbell and Pedersen 2001: 3): reforms have often been driven by force or expedience (Gibbon 1993); they have relied on hybrid or vernacular forms of authority (Schamis 1999); those social groups and classes threatened or marginalised by neoliberal reforms have contested them in a variety of ways (Mkandawire and Olukoshi 1995; Smith et al. 2008); the scheduling and funding of reform activities have been replete with game-playing, subterfuge and corruption (Mosley et al. 1995).

Research on neoliberal intervention has increasingly revealed the 'dirtiness' of reform – that is, its intermixing with non-neoliberal political practices. The faith that the simple rolling back of the state and the invisible hand would generate harmonious socio-economic recovery was short-lived (Gowan 1995). Subsequently – as we saw in Chapter 2 – contingent social support funds were introduced, not just because of concerns for reform 'losers' (Nelson 1990) but also in response to protests and riots against specific aspects of structural adjustment programmes. From the early 1990s, institutional form became a central concern of neoliberal intervention, focussing mainly on state capacity to promote, schedule, manage and audit neoliberal progress (Williams 1996). A little later, a concern with 'political will' emerged which expressed a growing and explicit awareness that reform agents were not necessarily individual instantiations of *Homo economicus* or *Homo rationalis* or neoliberal 'change agents'. Political will, reform progress and rates of economic growth have spurred a range of econometric rankings of countries undergoing neoliberal intervention, again suggesting that neoliberalism's progress is substantially dependent on aspects of local social and political patterning. All of these developments rendered critical studies of neoliberalism increasingly attuned not to the merits of the (sacred) model of neoliberalism but to the myriad vernaculars generated in different instances (Brenner and Theodore 2002). Indeed, most recently, for some the extent of 'dirtiness' within neoliberal reform has created such a degree of localism and diversity that the term 'neoliberalism' no longer usefully captures the essence of reform.

Recognising that neoliberalism's ideal-type and reform realities do not map onto each other at all well is in itself unremarkable. This is the essence of all grand projects of social engineering (Scott 1998). We can derive from this mismatch a sense of how ideologically driven intervention is, or highlight how 'politics' renders many of the designs of neoliberalism problematic in their execution. But, more intriguingly, the mismatch between the ideal and the concrete poses more challenging questions. Let us elaborate.

Reconciling the sacred and the profane

Neoliberal ontologies of agency are formulated through rational-choice approaches to agency. In a sense, rational choice is all about agency; its methodological individualism produces a range of models for individual action, often articulated through preferential thought experiments of prisoner's dilemmas, tragedies of the commons, and so on. Rational-choice modelling opens up space to look at people's actions, rather than seeing people as bearers of neoliberal structures-in-construction.

There is clearly some value to rational-choice approaches, as is recognised eloquently by some who are far away from neoliberalism on the political spectrum (Elster 1986). It is something of a truism that people have interests and preferences and that they are motivated to select and pursue those interests. But, as a way to bring agency into an analysis of neoliberal practice, rational-choice approaches to agency are partially useful at best. A number of questions have been raised about how one defines interests, how one uses econometric methodologies to aggregate up from the individual to the collective, and the general utilitarianism that rational choice creates at the expense of other normative frameworks. Here, we need to think specifically about the ontology of the rational-choice agent in terms of the repercussions for our conceptualisation of development practice in Africa.

Rational-choice approaches define agency not by its practices but by its interests. Interests produce alternative possible actions, which are then balanced through some kind of utilitarian summation, and therefrom – it is assumed – discrete actions emerge. It is striking, then, that although agency is central to rational choice, practice is not. To elaborate: rational-choice agency is understood as an outcome of rational calculations iterated constantly by individuals who are effectively determined by external questions that neoliberal economists consider to be constitutive. These questions are all based on neoliberal premisses; for example, what are the incentives that will make an agent more efficient (the key question of principal-agent theory)? To what extent does an institution replicate or conform to the free-market model (the key question of New Public Management)? How can freedom and rights be constructed to as to promote socially beneficial competition (New Institutional Economics)? Each of these questions – and their theoretical problem-solving frameworks – exists at the core of neoliberal practice in Africa.

Primarily, the World Bank understands political change and political agency with recourse to three approaches to political processes. In the first place, *rational choice* provides the lens through which social actors are perceived. Rational choice relies on an ontology of individual motivation through the pursuit of consciously held and ranked preferences. Society is thus an aggregation of individual preferences, perhaps bound by institutions or repeated games; states are institutions that structure the incentives of individual public functionaries and those of society more broadly. The Bank has embraced rational choice partly because of its normative affiliation with neoclassical economics, but also because it provides a robust theory of political agency. Thus the Bank supports projects to make 'citizen-users' (Pinto 1998: 389) more active in pressuring the state for 'value for money', mainly through service-delivery surveys. Both of these research projects were funded by the World Bank and the latter involved Bank staff in the research.

This feeds into the second theoretical point of origin – New Public Management (NPM) (McCourt and Minogue 2001). It is clear that NPM has not achieved an uncontested 'paradigmatic' status in public policy literature. It is not clear exactly to what extent NPM reforms have been rolled out in indebted states (Larbi 1995), but we can identify NPM as a key component in World Bank praxis. Here, the methodological individualism of rational choice feeds directly into a theory of public action. NPM is based on two basic claims: that the state should intervene in the economy as little as possible, and that state agents act to maximise their utility according to the structure of incentives in which they are embedded. Here we find very clear and direct praxis: public-sector reform programmes funded by the Bank and involving World Bank technical assistance have been focused on introducing competition into public service provision (agentisation, the tendering of services etc.; see World Bank 2000b), increasing transparency (public expenditure reviews, information-management systems, 'voice' mechanisms, whistle-blowing procedures etc.), and increasing public-service performance and efficiency by implementing clearer and more 'incentivised' rewards (performance management/review/appraisal, functional reviews, decompressed pay structures etc.; see World Bank 1999, 2004).

Between them, the closely related rational-choice and NPM approaches provide the Bank with a theory of political action and political agency: they direct the Bank towards specific kinds of reform and provide an argument about how political agencies will react to it. Political agency is essentially individualised and motivated by the balance of preferences, costs and benefits. Often, reforms are executed through the shaping of incentives and cost–benefit balances of an agent (an executing individual or department) by a principal (a head of unit or a minister) (Klitgaard 1989).

The third theoretical source for Bank action might be broadly termed institutionalism (Picciotto 1995; Klitgaard 1995; Harriss et al. 1995). Deriving from Douglass North's historical institutionalism, and appropriated by the World Bank through Joseph Stiglitz's research on transition economies (Stiglitz 1999), institutionalism brings the Bank's attention to the state in a way that is not simply concerned with minimising bureaucracy or introducing market proxies to administration (World Bank 2002). In essence, institutionalism focuses on the state as a market-complementing institution, with properties that are not replaceable by or analogous to the free market. In this vein, public-sector reform aims to 'provide the elements necessary for a well-functioning market economy' (World Bank 1994b: 13). States possess (or potentially possess) specific properties of information management, stability, development management and discipline. It is clear in both Stiglitz and North that the salience of institutions derives from their complementarity to market social relations as it does for the Bank. Thus, there is no radical disjuncture from neoliberalism implied by the embracing of institutionalism by the Bank, but institutionalism does provide new properties to political change and agency for the Bank, most notably a kind of revived statism (Moore 1999). The Bank has funded various reforms that contain institutionalist thinking: information management projects, capacity building of one kind or another, and training. The Bank was a key donor to the African Capacity Building Initiative, which maintains very close ties with the World Bank (World Bank 1995; World Bank Public Sector Board 2000b; Akuoko-Frimpong 1994: 19).

In sum, we can identify three approaches that provide the intellectual resources for the Bank's governance operations in African states. In contrast to identifying higher levels of abstracted theory, rational choice, new public management and institutionalism provide approaches that relate more closely to how the Bank perceives its own actions to prosecute reform and give a clearer idea of what the Bank expects of its reforms – in other words, how it expects reforms to work themselves through African states. In this sense, these three approaches give us a picture of how the Bank sees African states and the agencies that drive them: projects are executed by 'champions', 'change teams' or principals, well trained, motivated and paid to implement changes to others' incentive structures through a modification of rewards and a greater flow of information, which also introduces aspects of competition and efficiency to public service.

It is for this reason that neoliberal studies of agency are replete with liberal market metaphors concerning calculative rationality and utility maximisation in place of any other sociological understandings of agency (Fine 2000). This kind of approach allows us to look at concrete neoliberal interventions, but it leaves us with a rather emaciated understanding of agency. Interests are defined by outcomes and judged by the standards of a neoliberal *a priori* of utilitarian calculative rationality. What if the connections between intentions, actions and outcomes are less robust? How do we account for the ways in which practices of neoliberalism are not discrete iterations but are strongly embedded in already-existing traditions and institutions? Isn't it possible that there are various kinds of interests bubbling within social practices, many of which are imperfectly realised and perhaps even not mutually consistent with each other? These kinds of questions suggest an altogether more complex kind of neoliberal intervention, one that might well lose the clarity of the approach outlined above. But it also suggests a far more involved and central role for agency in our understandings of neoliberal reform – not an agency that serves as an individualised vehicle for the calculative rationality of the free-market model, but an agency that is conscious of practices as a richer realisation of individual action: embedded, normatively interpolated and reflexive. In this sense, social practice is not a measure of neoliberal progress but rather how the latter is constituted *tout court*.

Furthermore, the neoliberal understanding of agency is purposefully formulated as a metric, a way of understating the extent of – and limits to – reform progress. As such, neoliberal analysis contains an endpoint according to which concrete acts and processes are evaluated. This teleological tendency doesn't interprets existing agencies on their own terms; rather, it uses rational-choice techniques to evaluate the extent to which these agencies resemble – or are likely to resemble – a market-like condition. Indeed, neoliberal ontology serves to construct and realise the norms of the market (Tsakalotos 2005).

Pragmatism and neoliberalism

The previous section has argued that our understanding of neoliberalism profoundly conditions our understanding of development practice. Indeed, neoliberalism's intellectual purchase has largely derived not from its constitutive features – these are very close to common-or-garden and generic definitions of capitalism – but from its *dynamics*; that is, its existence as a project to transform selves, institutions and societies (e.g. Harvey 2005; Peck and Tickell 2002). We have seen that neoliberal perceptions of agency have been based on a tension between the sacred and profane in which neoliberalism is endowed with an agency *sui generis*, or discrete 'neoliberal acts' are seen as working in the interests of a neoliberal *telos*. Also, in our discussion of critical definitions of neoliberalism, we found other difficulties with the role of agency within neoliberalism – either as a result of an endowing of neoliberalism with agency itself, or a reliance on a 'backwards reading' of reform as serving previously defined interests.

This section will set out a more deeply agency-centred way of understanding neoliberal intervention based on theories of pragmatism. The conceptual tools that one might derive from this theoretical approach will be used in the subsequent chapters to demonstrate how we might understand neoliberal intervention in sub-Saharan Africa.

The rather stylised distinction between the sacred and the profane (cf. Geschiere and Nyamnjoh 2000: 444) used so far is in fact familiar to the pragmatist tradition. John Dewey uses a distinction between the holy and profane in his discussion of social rupture and uncertainty (Dewey 1929: 11). This seems apposite because neoliberal reforms have produced a great deal of uncertainty (Bourdieu 1993) and in some circumstances 'peril' (to borrow Dewey's own phrase). Much of Dewey's discussion of 'peril' is analogous to our discussion above. He argues that in situations of uncertainty, some ordinary acts become endowed with unusual power (fortune) and become read as working 'in favour of some overshadowing power' (1929: 12). This seems reasonably in keeping with the ways in which acts are interpreted through a neoliberal *telos*, a filtering or translation of the efficacy of acts according to the extent to which their results advance a neoliberal end-state. In Dewey's view, 'practical affairs ... are relatively low, secular and profane compared with the perfect realities of rational science' (1929: 27). It seems, then, that pragmatism is based on a rejection of the kind of reification neoliberal analysis relies upon.

Dewey goes on to argue that the reified distinction between knowledge (magical or otherwise) and action is a fundamental problem for our understanding of acts of social reform, and this provides the *raison d'être* for the development of pragmatist theories of social action. So, if it appears that pragmatist theory is based on an unhappiness with any understanding of agency based on external *a priori* frameworks of value (knowledge), what kind of approach to agency might we derive as an alternative? Here, I wish to focus mainly on Dewey's work because it is fundamental to the pragmatist tradition and because his work seems to me to be potentially very useful in developing a way of understanding neoliberal interventions with fuller attention given to agency.

The core of Dewey's pragmatism is a rejection of ontological separations between ideas and practice not simply because they are not separate, but more positively because they are mutually constitutive or, perhaps better, part of a unity. In other words, ideas and actions are co-produced through a range of social properties which seem very familiar: reflection, evaluation, habit, intention, sense and so on. This is a valuable way of moving beyond dyads of ideas and experience/practice because it brings our attention towards not only the ways practice is produced as discrete acts but also the premises and prospectives of these acts. Practices produce knowledge; knowledge enables ideas; ideas serve to create intentions for practices. This is not to impute some kind of virtuous circularity to social practice; rather, it is to show how a focus on practice necessarily requires attention to both acts and the ideas that are embedded in those acts. In the pragmatist tradition, there is no 'raw' or empirical action; rather, action is reflective, based in judgements and socially interpolated.

But this is merely a starting point, a shift in focus. We need to think about how this point of departure might serve to analyse such a grand project as neoliberalism. What we must recognise first is that an attention to practice is not empiricism; pragmatism is not concerned solely to describe and categorise actions and ideas. Rather, Dewey and his epigones have seen pragmatism as a way of thinking heuristically about practice. That is, because practice is social and infused with ideas, values, and so on, it is important to try to *interpret* practice through broader understandings of society and power. Neoliberalism is one such candidate for a broader understanding. It provides coordinates – nothing more – to make sense of social practices which are *sui generis*. If those practices do not fit the coordinates, this requires us to rethink our coordinates (Castree 2006).

Conduct, habit, repertoire

This is where the concepts of habit, conduct and repertoire are apposite. These three concepts – only loosely taken from Dewey – serve as 'meso', mid-range, or grounded (generally, Elster 1986: 17; regarding neoliberalism, see Campbell and Pedersen 2001: 27; Castree 2006) concepts that allow us to 'think upwards' from practices to a more ambitious sense-making. They allow us the possibility of critically analysing neoliberalism as a project constituted by myriad practices rather than market ideals or the teleology of rational progress. The three terms – habit, conduct and repertoire – are initially categorical but also heuristic; they allow us to bundle practices together with the aim of interpreting their significance outside of their immediate realm. Let us take each concept in turn and flesh out what kind of work they do.

Although Dewey uses the term 'conduct' in the title of one of his key books concerning social practice (1929), he does not fully explain the term, moving on to other more specific concerns. However, in the introduction he discusses morality in a way that sets up his study of human nature in terms of how we evaluate conduct, 'an order of judgements' which enable interrelated practices (Dewey, in Campbell 1995: 110). It is along these lines that we use the term here: a recognition that activities are always moral as well as materially 'effective' in some sense. In familiar terms, one might think of how the word 'conduct' is used in general discourse: at school, in terms of good or bad conduct; or in phrases such as 'she conducted herself well'. These kinds of usage resonate with that employed here – conduct as the moral import of action.

This is not to set up some form of universal standard by which to make normative commentary on social practice – external criteria of good and bad conduct. This would bring us back to the kind of universal progressivism that underpins neoliberalism as a world-view. Rather, the moral content of actions should be seen in the first instance as immanent; that is, actions as containing their own moral statements or claims that are articulated within a specific social sphere in which 'the make-up and working of human forces afford a basis for moral ideas and ideals' (Dewey 1922: 8) within the 'cultural and political-economic processes of intricate, grounded domains' (Kingfisher and Maskovsky 2008: 120). Practice establishes conduct, in that it is an intrinsic part of human action that it is normatively infused. Thus, pragmatism can establish a kind of relativism (Rorty 1993) based on a respect for social practice and the social realms it creates (Festenstein 2002). This simply means that conduct is not a universal; it is a component of all practices which are, in some sense and in the first instance, vernacular (Kymlicka 2001).

Habit is a phrase used by Dewey, although he is shy of giving it a clear definition. What he is focusing on, however, is iteration. Clearly, a great deal of social practice is in part undertaken because something like it has been undertaken before. Social practices which have generated their own facility are habits; they are fairly stable in the ways that ends and means are connected and the ways in which these intentions and outcomes are thought through. To some degree, one might connect the notion of habit with another wing of pragmatism, that derived from Pierre Bourdieu (1977) and his concept of habitus, but I would not want to define habit in a way that is highly structured because this concept tends to de-emphasise agency (Hodgson 2004; Weiss 2004: 199). Nevertheless, habitual practice is in some sense stabilising even if it is not a structure or inertia. In Dewey's view, habits emerge as those who act in a certain realm need to deal with uncertainty and contingency; in this sense there is a tension in which habits have to reassert themselves and likely modify themselves in the face of changes.

The notion of repertoires derives from Dewey's key question concerning ideas in action: 'what determines the selection of operations to be performed?' (1929: 123). Thus far, we have specified a pragmatist approach as focusing on practices as generative of ideas and knowledge. We have outlined how practice can be understood as morally infused and also embedded in precedent, both of which emphasise Dewey's concern with reflective action – 'experimental inquiry or thinking signifies *directed activity*' (Dewey 1922: 123) – which is at the heart of a Deweyan understanding of human agency. The addition of repertoire to this framework is simply to recognise that no agency is unconstrained in the choices of action made – the 'constraints on the range of solutions that actors perceive and deem useful for solving problems' (Campbell 2001: 170). Indeed some courses of action will be a lot more likely than others as a result of the ways in which people evaluate existing practices, likely outcomes and senses of good or bad action. This means that repertoire does not simply connote a toolbox of techniques (for example, the various ways in which a government might transfer management of public enterprises to the private sector) but rather that agents recognise – and to some extent create – a series of 'realistic' alternative ways of acting through reflection.

That these choices are constrained is precisely why we need to consider these three terms as working at a 'meso' level. The nature of constraint is not simply internal to a realm of practice; it is also, and very importantly, external in the sense that interventions from elsewhere aim to change practice by changing repertoires. This is the essence of social engineering: neoliberal intervention aims to destabilise existing habits (expressed within neoliberal discourse as a hostility to bureaucracy and a desire for good governance, for example) and to produce notions of conduct based on efficiency, transparency and utility. It also aims to destabilise existing conduct by producing values of efficiency, transparency, value for money, and so on, within states that are likely to work according to different forms of conduct (Bayart 1993). It also aims to render some possible actions easier, more rewarding or more obvious than others.

The argument here is that social practices in Africa have experienced a tangible destabilisation as a result of neoliberal intervention mainly but not exclusively aimed at the state. As a result, the 'lived history' of neoliberalism – that which is realised through practices of adaption, adoption, resistance and subterfuge – can be found in the ways social practice has changed within those many African states that have undergone decades of neoliberal intervention.

But one final question faces us before we move on: how do we move from the meso to the macro? Or, more specifically, how do we relate bundles of practice to the project of global neoliberalism? The answer is, at best, suggestive, and cannot be more that that without becoming (in my view at least) excessively deterministic – a danger that is replete within studies of neoliberalism, as I have already argued above. The nub of the issue resides in the bundling itself: the intellectual effort to relate discrete practices in order to think interpretively about the nature of those practices and the kinds of change that they usher in. Again, this is a point made strongly by Dewey in his efforts to distinguish pragmatism from empiricism, and we can quote him at length:

> There are specific good reasons for the usual attribution of acts to the person from whom they immediately proceed. But to convert this special reference into a belief of exclusive ownership is as misleading

as to suppose that breathing and digesting are complete within the human body. To get a rational basis for moral discussion we must begin with recognising that functions ... are ways of using and incorporating the environment in which the latter has its say as surely as the former. (1922: 15)

In essence, 'moral discussion' – or perhaps, in more contemporary language, critical analysis – requires us to 'think upwards' towards the larger systems ('environments') within which bundles of practices are situated. This has been the methodology throughout the book: to identify practices that have emerged during the neoliberal period, to think explicitly and heuristically about how they can be bundled together, and finally to relate upwards to the generics of neoliberalism not as a way of determining the importance and nature of the practices, but rather as *determining the importance and nature of neoliberalism itself.*

This chapter has set out the value of a pragmatist approach to neoliberal social engineering in the attention it pays to practice as a political phenomenon. We also set out three aspects of practice regarding how neoliberalism might infuse social practices throughout Africa in ways that enable us to identify a global project. This sets a frame of reference for the next three chapters: to look at changing practices and to move between the meso and macro levels. As such, the aim is not so much to present a detailed set of empirical observations about individuals' practices but rather to look at how neoliberal habit, repertoires and conduct have changed within international institutions, states and other social groups. The next three chapters look at the international, national and local levels respectively.

4

Global neoliberal practice:
institutions and regulation

THIS CHAPTER considers the global emergence of neoliberalism. It looks at the ways in which neoliberal practice has emerged, expanded and established for itself 'paradigmatic' status. In other words, it shows how neoliberalism has shifted from an ambitious and embryonic set of policy interventions to something resembling a framework or set of premisses within which policy is articulated. The practices of neoliberalism have been iterated over such time as to shift the habits, conduct and repertoire of development practice *tout court*. The layering of large numbers of neoliberal policies has not only led to a progressively more totalising implementation of liberalisation; it has also defined the terms upon which policy and development are thought about and articulated per se. This is, of course, not a completed process (in the last chapter we developed a framework which is anathema to the idea of completed processes, preferring instead a series of practices in place of means–ends distinctions), but it has enabled neoliberal ideas to aspire to 'meta-development' status: that is, as the terms upon which development is discussed rather than solely as a predominant model of development. At the level of ideas, this shift or tendency is rather like the analysis of Hay in which neoliberalism moves from normalising to normative (Hay 2004).

Thus, this chapter concerns itself with neoliberalism at the international level – its history of ratcheting up the ambitions of liberalisation since the late 1970s. But, there is a danger here. As suggested in chapters 1 and 3, it is this kind of concern that most tempts writers to endow neoliberalism with agency. After all, it is at the global-historical level that neoliberalism seems to be an idea that *does* shape history. Furthermore, at the global level, any project to identify the substantially more complex realm of agency and practice will very quickly produce a certain degree of bewilderment: neoliberalism has been realised through a nebulous, formal and semi-formal, and complex series of meetings, rule-setting, lending mechanisms, research outputs and exertions of political pressure. In this sense, abstracting an idea-agency called neoliberalism to encompass the global sweep towards liberalisation seems very tempting. However, it is not the task of this book to detail a global history of neoliberal practice. Our focus is on neoliberal practice in Africa and this necessarily takes us centrally to African states and questions of development policy practice. Therefore, what we need to do in this chapter is to narrate the key developments in the expansion of neoliberalism, but with a wariness of allowing neoliberalism to 'take flight' and become history in itself.

This chapter will analyse the international construction of neoliberal regulation in this spirit. It pays particular attention to institutional change and the emergence of neoliberal norms of regulation. This serves to foreground vital aspects of the repertoire of development practice in African states.

Global neoliberalism: free markets and political power

Persistent practice

The last twenty years have witnessed the globalisation of neo-liberal economic reform, from specific electoral victories in the

United States and Britain to the 'common sense' that lies more or less implicitly behind the thought and action of practically all states and international organisations (Robison 2006; Demmers et al. 2004). Through a range of processes, post-communist states, post-colonial states, the international finance institutions and UN agencies have all cleaved to the same neoliberal fundamentals (Demmers et al. 2004; Fine et al. 2001; Lee and McBride 2007; Roy et al. 2007). A rough but revealing expression of this can be found in the narrowing of questions in international development discourse: no longer questions about the relative merits of market and non-market forms of economic organisation, but how to make the expansion of the market work for the poor; no longer questions about the comparative benefits of public or private ownership, but how to make privatisation more efficient (McDonald and Ruiters 2005). How did this happen?

The global economic slowdown of the 1970s, accompanied by increasing instability and the heightened class tensions within many national contexts, created an enabling environment for politicians, intellectuals and policymakers to develop the foundations of neoliberal ideas and practices – what might retrospectively be called first-generation neoliberalism (circa 1979–95) (see, for example, the reflections of Williamson 2000).

First-generation neoliberalism was prosecuted by a group of intellectuals who had espoused critiques of the pre-existing ideas of regulation, social democracy and statist development. These critiques had persisted throughout the post-war period (Bauer 1972), and indeed many staff in the IMF cleaved to notions of monetarism, economic liberalism and anti-statism. What emerged in the early 1980s was an *enabling* of neoliberal ideas (Brett 2008: 340). The IMF attained an increasingly dominant and aggressive role as macroeconomic keeper of economies in increasingly dire straits (Havnevik 1987). The party ideological atmosphere in many economically powerful Western states moved to the right, lending the 'free market' a revived ideological cachet

(Turner 2008). Economic recession created a context in which development orthodoxies looked increasingly fragile and alternative – even radical – solutions became increasingly thinkable. This was because the global slowdown and instability of the late 1970s could be readily shaped as a crisis of Keynesian and developmental approaches (whatever the precise linkages between social democratic or statist-nationalist paradigms and 'crisis') and alternative approaches advocated.

We can readily see that the early 1980s was a period of tensions and mismatches between political institutions, class relations and patterns of socio-economic interaction. Duménil and Lévy (2001, 2004) demonstrate how the 1970s had produced a fall in rates of profit, which put pressure on capital and states to disempower workers and reduce labour's influence over government, particularly in favour of finance capital. Kotz (2008) also focuses on the shifting institutional forms that neoliberal regimes produce, arguing that governments attempted to address economic decline and profit squeeze by removing controls on capital, adjusting fiscal policy in favour of capital, and putting the state more forcefully to work to support finance, property and capital mobility.

What these analyses show us is how structural shifts in the global economy were realised through a series of interrelated debates and policy changes in many states and international organisations that enabled advocates of economic liberalisation to shape the direction of economic orthodoxy towards the practices and premisses of neoliberalism. This was not an inevitability; it was a piecemeal and contested project. The 1980s proved to be an extremely turbulent decade, characterised by attempts to liberalise, resistance against the latter, reform 'slippage' and indeed in some cases social collapse, not only in Africa but in myriad ways throughout the world (Kozul-Wright and Rayment 2007; Bond 2004; Fisher and Ponniah 2003).

Within an enduring state of economic sluggishness and social turbulence, the persistence of the intellectuals and practitioners of liberalisation maintained an open field for neoliberal practice. In the absence of a powerful rival set of practices and ideas, neoliberalism became in this strict sense 'necessary', and its repeated failure to stabilise societies or reinvigorate the global economy did not so much disempower the advocates of neoliberalism (whose numbers were growing) as much as harden and recapitulate neoliberal practice. This is perhaps the historic import of Margaret Thatcher's apocryphal phrase 'there is no alternative'. Neoliberal practice was endlessly asserted despite its inability to produce stable growth and social peace (Chapter 2) because it had no alternatives that so effectively conjoined ideology and policy practice.

Dark victories

At the time when Walden Bello used the phrase 'dark victories' (Bello 1993), there was a sense that neoliberalism was being imposed on suffering societies in ways that were nothing short of coercive. That this neoliberal project brought much hardship and political turbulence is both evident and unsurprising. However, efforts to implement neoliberalism have endured the 1980s, bringing in new policies and modes of intervention. This has led some to speak of a twofold sequencing of neoliberal implementation: first- and second-generation reform. First generation-reform (FGR) is characterised as being a period of compulsory adjustment to market 'realities'; second-generation reform (SGR) is seen as a subsequent and less troubled period in which the 'basics' (some version of the Washington Consensus) are in place and it remains to use these basics as the guidelines for broader projects of social engineering – within both states (Chapter 5) and societies (Chapter 6). The notions of first- and second-generation reform are in a sense misleading: this stadial account of neoliberal implementation gives a sense of a completed first stage followed by a more sophisticated second stage. This leads us to a teleology, functionalism and consequentialism again. For those advocating neoliberalism, the presence of second-generation reform is evidence that a state has 'graduated' beyond the basics of fiscal discipline and liberalised prices. It enables bolder and more expansive neoliberal practice under the assumption that a 'critical velocity' or 'fundamentals' have been attained, in which resistance and recidivism against neoliberalism have been bypassed.

However, there is a way in which the distinction between first- and second-generation reform is analytically useful. This is to highlight the process already sketched in the section above: a tendency for neoliberal ideas not only to produce powerful models of development but also to *produce development itself.* As an expanding bundle of practices, neoliberalism's second-generation status is premissed on the *political* consolidation of a 'common sense'. The common sense that SGR requires is that first-generation reforms are both in place and uncontested. This is aptly encapsulated by the World Bank in its millennial *Development Report*:

> Supporting good policies is important but it is not enough. We learned in the 1990s that process is as important as policy.... The way donors and recipients interact strongly influences the effectiveness of development co-operation. Relationships have tended to follow the preferences of donor countries, leaving recipients with little sense of ownership.... If development co-operation is to attack poverty effectively and efficiently, donors will need to ... provide sustained support for policy and institutional environments. (World Bank 2000/2001: 191–2)

In the *World Development Report* of 1997, the World Bank sets out a model of first- and second-generation reforms in which the latter are seen as constituted in 'deep institutional reforms', moving out of 'enclaves' of reform to entire public institutions (World Bank 1997: 152–3).

This section maps out this movement, from persistent and combative practice towards (but never completing) consensual paradigm. The section is nothing more than a sketch; more detail will be provided in following sections that look more closely at institutional practice and interaction.

Despite the unstable condition of neoliberal policies throughout the world, the 1980s witnessed a profusion of more-or-less short-lived neoliberal experiments. As argued in Chapter 1, this African experience represents an extreme image of a global process of purposeful neoliberal implementation. In Chapter 2 we saw how fragile the evidence was of 'success' during the first decade of neoliberal reform. This allowed us to highlight the persistence and determination of largely Western advocates of neoliberalism. But 'success' and 'failure' premiss themselves on a simplistic means–ends distinction which removes our focus on the development of reform habits constituted by practices. In this sense, what the 1980s show are iterations: repeated and modified exactions to liberalise and reconfigure development management. Thus, the profusion of SAP produced increasingly integrated and institutionally complex practices of implementation *regardless* of the fragile and unstable economic growth that characterised the decade. So, how did the institutions of neoliberal implementation emerge?

In spite of some distinctions and differences between the two Bretton Woods Institutions, the World Bank and the IMF accustomed themselves to working in close coordination throughout the 1980s (Taylor 1997). The consolidation of neoliberalism has been effected through the growth of a powerful and nebulous international structure of publicly constituted regulative authority. The World Bank, largely due to the implementation of a regime of structural adjustment in the global South, transformed itself from a project-lending international bank to a key influence within policymaking and macroeconomic management throughout the developing world (Please 1984). The IMF moved from short-term exchange-rate creditor to policy-based lender as well, and has also acted to lend large tranches of conditional dollars to emerging market economies experiencing currency crashes.

We will come back to these developments in more detail in the next section. The point here is to signal that the global rise of neoliberalism has involved the elaboration of a new international

architecture of regulation, still very much in construction (Soederberg 2002a, 2002b). The age of neoliberalism is characterised by
two closely interrelated, but apparently conflicting trends: a powerful consolidation of neoliberal economic fundamentals based on
rolling back the state and 'freeing' the market; and the generation
of a powerful international institutional network of *public* authority,
bound together more or less formally through a policy consensus
on issues such as macroeconomic reform, anti-corruption measures
and trade policy. One can frame this as a paradox: an integrated
ascendance of international public institutions to usher in a 'marketised' global order. But, from a pragmatist point of view, this
paradox is only apparent. Because all development practice is
political, it is a logical impossibility to imagine an unregulated
social practice. In this light, liberalisation can only be understood as a bundle of actions which attempt to create novel habits
– in other words, different regulative effects. Thus, implementing
liberalisation is simply the international practice of neoliberalism
with specific attention to the 'first-generation' efforts to replace
previous habits.

Implementing liberalisation, imposing practice

From 1980 onwards, the World Bank would develop an progressively
more pervasive and detailed set of conditional lending mechanisms
under the rubric of SAP. Although these SAPs would vary in some
degree between countries, it was certainly the case that all were
based on a desire to liberalise economies. The drive of SAP in its
early implementation was to remove price subsidies within internal
markets, to abolish quotas, and to allow exchange rates to float
freely. Beyond these core components, all SAPs would also involve
policy commitments to many of the following: privatisation, tariff
reduction, the removal of state marketing boards, reducing money
supply with a view to reducing inflation, encouraging foreign
investment, reducing the government payroll, and introducing

user charges for public services. Each of these specific aspects of reform, especially when taken collectively, reveal how the World Bank employed loan conditionalities to remove the state from the economy and to provide more freedom to the workings of market signals and capital.

This in itself is well known and hardly contentious. Indeed, the World Bank repeatedly and explicitly represents itself as promoting marketisation through its macroeconomic policy-based lending. What this section aims to do is simply map how this liberalising drive, encoded into SAPs, was also integrated into a broader and extremely powerful network of international institutions.

From the 1980s, the IMF's lending also became conditional on liberalisation. For the IMF, this was less of a change in policy than it was for the World Bank: the IMF had been concerned with macroeconomic indices since its inception. What was more significant was the expansion in the IMF's remit and its emerging role as lead agency in a constellation of external advocates of neo-liberalism. The IMF's chief concern was the stability of exchange rates, and it lent money to countries that needed to adjust rates to reflect their 'real' (that is, market-determined) value. During the 1980s, the IMF incorporated a series of macroeconomic 'headlines' concerning budget deficits, rates of inflation and currency devaluation into its concerns. The IMF's role complemented the World Bank's in that it lent to lock in and stabilise discrete adjustments to baseline macroeconomic reforms, whereas the World Bank maintained a focus on more programmatic and 'developmental' aspects of reform, for example encouraging foreign investment or reforming public services. In practice, the World Bank and the IMF worked closely together and their respective remits became increasingly indistinct, not least because these two institutions worked together in each country setting.

The IMF also developed an increasingly powerful role as auditor. Again, this was not entirely novel: the IMF had a long-standing role as a respected 'scientific' institution which produced statistics on national economies. What emerged in the 1980s was that key economic indices (inflation, interest rates, current account deficits, exchange rates) became the material through which the World Bank and the IMF would rank-order national economies according to the extent that they had liberalised. It also provided an evidential base for the IMF to categorise states according to their progress in neoliberal reform. Those countries in a state of delinquency would raise concerns not only for the IMF or the World Bank, but also a raft of other international agencies, bilateral, multilateral, private and public. 'Off track' would lead to frozen or cancelled grants or loans, and a likely adjusting down of other indices concerned with investment risk and creditworthiness, as ten countries were in the early 2000s, with Zambia undergoing severe delays in the release of tranches (Jubilee Research 2003: 18). The World Bank also produces rankings according to Country Policy and Institutional Assessments, which evaluate six aspects of policy, much of which clearly translates into a fealty to neoliberal reform. Again, these indicators affect donor and perhaps also international companies' interest in any specific country. And, if the latter require more neoliberal rank-orderings of potential sites for investment, the Bank also offers a 'Doing Business Index' which is, again, entirely dedicated to the rights of property.

Liberalisation was also pursued – albeit awkwardly – through trade reforms, largely through the final GATT round. This final round – dubbed the Uruguay Round – aimed to agree a range of principles that would then usher in a new institution: the World Trade Organisation. The WTO was designed to produce a universal and semi-independent body to ensure equal treatment between trading nations and a progressive ratcheting down of tariffs, non-preference and other controls of trade – not only in goods but also in services and knowledge. Thus, we can see that neoliberalism emerged centrally through the increasing prominence of the World Bank and the IMF and their use of conditionality effectively to define the repertoire of social and economic policy.

From these core institutions, a raft of international institutions have developed a series of neoliberal practices. These practices are not perfect scientific instruments to forge a global market society: like all practice, neoliberal practice is 'dirtied' by individual dispositions, institutional traditions and cultural forms. Nevertheless, one can discern the 'momentum' incorporated into these practices – the movement towards a neoliberal social order – and one can also identify interlinkages that bind discrete practices together. As a bundle of practices, neoliberalism can be seen as a global project in which each specific reform, intervention and initiative gains a 'value added' in terms of its purchase or effectiveness by virtue of its affirmation of the broad sway of programmatic and policy change.

The rest of this chapter looks at the emergence of this bundle of practices as a historically constructed and multilevel phenomenon. It does so with particular attention to the World Bank, partly because of the salience of this institution as a producer of development practice and also because the World Bank has been the key agency in neoliberal intervention in Africa.

The World Bank and Africa

By the time of the second OPEC oil-price hike in 1979, the developmental project was in tatters. Levels of debt had become sufficiently high to make it difficult to imagine how some states could *ever* escape from indebtedness. The international economy, which had expanded constantly during the 1960s and slowed in the 1970s, was now clearly in recession. The 'long downturn' (Brenner 1998: 138ff.) that commenced in 1973 was addressed from 1979 by a strong shift towards monetarist economic management within the United States and the UK, with other states moving (more or less willingly – see especially France in 1981) in a similar direction over the next decade or so. Perhaps an initial event which starkly announced the shift in the 'policy logic' of regulation was the substantial rises in interest rates from 1979 in the USA, which in turn had severe recessionary effects in the West (Brenner 2001: 24ff.).

Globally, the rise of economic liberalism produced a radical change in forms of regulation. The IFIs came under strong pressure – especially from the USA (Wade and Veneroso 1998) – to act as institutions to consolidate and 'lock in' a neoliberal architecture. As already argued, the neoliberal project has involved just as much concerted political intervention as did the previous embedded liberal project, which is why Gill (1995) calls is disciplinary neoliberalism. The IFIs increased their capacity to intervene and invigilate, remaking themselves as the active champions of the regulative revolution, reframing 'development' as liberalisation and bringing this ideology into the indebted states of the world. There was no region of the world more vulnerable to these global regulative changes than Africa (Abrahamsen 2000).

The economic slowdown in the West produced magnified crisis and vulnerability in the global South, especially Africa. Recession in Western economies dampened demand for primary commodity exports from the post-colonial economies, creating a decline in Africa's external terms of trade from 160.2 in 1980 to 110.5 in 1990 (base year 1995 – 100; Table 5–17 in World Bank 2000a). Sub-Saharan Africa's share of foreign direct investment declined from its already very marginal levels. Total external debt increased from $61 billion in 1980 to $177 billion in 1990, imposing severe pressure on public expenditures – social spending declined by 26 per cent from 1980 to 1985 (Riley and Parfitt 1994: 139). The details of the crisis that this produced in Africa are complex. Szeftel summarises as follows: 'The crisis of accumulation which has beset the world capitalist order [since the debt crisis] ... has been particularly severe in its impact on the poorest and most peripheral societies' (1987: 87). Metaphors such as the 'lost decade' of the 1980s and the 'death of development' signal the evaporation of purposive public action and a succession of ad hoc and crisis-management measures.

Thus, the incipient tensions of the previous period were brought to a conclusion in the form of a general economic recession, producing nothing short of a development crisis in many African countries. The Bank could no longer continue project lending to political economies that were reaching economic and social crisis. The result was a change in Bank strategy, starkly presented in the 'Berg Report' mentioned in Chapter 1 (World Bank 1981), and closely integrated into the rise of neoliberalism after 1979 in the West (Stern and Ferreira 1997: 537ff.). The 'Berg Report' set out a critique of the post-colonial state as a bloated, rent-seeking set of institutions which distorted price mechanisms in order to feather the nests of political elites. The solution was, in simple terms: less state, more market.

This overarching new agenda was implemented through the creation of structural adjustment lending in 1980. Moving from project support to support for macroeconomic restructuring, the Bank lent on the condition that states would implement the new orthodoxies of neoliberal economics: low rates of inflation, devaluation, high rates of interest, divestment of state property, an economy open to global markets and capital, and a general reduction in public expenditure. In essence, the fragility of African states after 1979 created an unprecedented opportunity for external regulative intervention, expressed through those institutions most heavily involved in sub-Saharan Africa: the World Bank and (later) the IMF.

SAPs were effected through the mechanism of conditionality: credit would only be forthcoming if governments implemented the 'correct' policies. This produced a very different relationship between the World Bank and indebted states to that of the debt-led development model.

The conditionality mechanism created considerable tension between governing elites and the Bank. In Tanzania during the early 1980s the tension between conditionality and the government was most clear in Nyerere's resistance to the devaluation of the Tanzanian shilling, manifested in his broadsides against the IMF (or the 'International Ministry of Finance', as he dubbed it) (Campbell and Stein 1992). Similar tensions between African governments and the IFIs existed throughout Africa, manifest in the tendency of 'adjusting' states to evade or abandon the policy reforms that the Bank and Fund made conditions of loans (Mosley et al. 1995).

Finally, it is vital to note that adjustment did not usher in any clear signs of economic recovery in sub-Saharan Africa (Mosley and Weeks 1993; Schatz 1994; Weeks 2001: 271). Perhaps one of the most successful intended consequences of structural adjustment was the erosion of (formal) state capacity, the effect of which was to make management of the economy and society increasingly difficult (Moore 1998). In sum, imposing neoliberalism produced its own delegitimising contradictions: it was effective as a strategy to ensure a global revolution in development thinking, but it failed as a strategy of economic development.

In sum, the 1980s encapsulated an effort to resolve the problems of economic slowdown and a weakening of global regulative architecture, manifest from 1973. The shift towards neoliberalism attempted to re-establish profitability as a prerequisite to reinvigorated growth. It produced a political and institutional response from the IFIs (strongly pushed forward by the USA) which established neoliberalism as a near-synonym for 'development' (described as meta-development earlier) and, through its own techniques of intervention, attempted to universalise neoliberal reform throughout a wide range of states facing more or less severe economic crisis.

But the 1980s was *not* a period of harmonisation – far from it. It was clear that the neoliberal revolution failed to legitimise itself within the states of the global South: it produced economic instability, was perceived as an external imposition (demonising the World Bank and the IMF in the process), and made indebted economies increasingly extroverted to a hostile global economy.

It is the *failure* of the neoliberal project of the 1980s that has led the World Bank and others to innovate a new regime of development, based on the 'post-Washington Consensus', governance and poverty reduction.

The contemporary global architecture of development

From the 1980s neoliberalism has pervaded all forms of international regulation, making imposition less pressing than reproduction and consolidation. This is the conjuncture that produced the so-called post-Washington Consensus (PWC). The PWC constitutes a rubric for a range of innovations that have a common purpose in imagining the social embeddedness of the free market (Sorensen 1991). Thus, we have information-theoretic economics and institutionalism (Fine et al. 2001), social capital (Edwards 1999), civil society (Landell Mills 1992), and governance (Williams 1996). Each of these themes contributes to a model of a society in which people act as self-interested individuals, harmonise their actions through information exchange and commonly accepted rules (either established in law or through 'trust'), and generate positive-sum effects in the polity and economy by respecting each other's rights. States rule transparently under the principal motivation of promoting the social relations of the market and the participation of the citizenry in that project. In contradistinction to the previous periods, these ideas collectively produce a discourse that represents neoliberal markets as embedded in societies. There is no rejection of liberalisation, but there is a central concern with how the state manages and schedules liberalisation, as well as 'an emphasis on the non-economic "glue" that holds society together' (Fine et al. 2001: xiii). The projects of the contemporary regulative architecture is to secure development – still forged in neoliberal fundamentals – in its relegitimisation through the post-Washington Consensus.

Embedding neoliberalism requires a bold repertoire of intervention and an epic vision – requirements that the World Bank has been aspiring to (Cammack 2002; Williams 1999; Cahn 1993; Einhorn 2001). Most writers generally accept that the period of embedded *liberalism*, say from 1958 to 1968, represented a period during which capitalism was successfully managed through an intermeshing of domestic and international regulation, underpinned by expansive national and global economies. However one understands the (brief) 'golden age' of capitalism, its *relative* success seems plainly clear: Milanovic's (2003) recent and sharp critique of celebratory accounts of globalisation is explicitly juxtaposed against the 'golden age' as a period of more expansive and developmental capitalism. 'Something is clearly wrong' with contemporary globalisation, he concludes (2003: 679).

As Robert Wade has shown, these interests can produce forms of regulation which are detrimental to development strategies (Wade 2003). Debt and trade structures systematically disadvantage weak states that rely on primary exports for hard currency. The figures exemplify some of the economics of Western dominance of the neoliberal agenda: from 1992 to 1998 Highly Indebted Poor Countries transferred $5.8 billion to the World Bank over what they received in new loans and credits (Pettifor and Garrett 2000); First World countries impose 50 per cent higher import barriers against the Third World than they do among themselves (Nares 1997: 18); Africa's income fell by about 2 per cent as a result of the conclusion of the Uruguay Round (Stiglitz 2002: 61); ODA from the West fell by 50 per cent between 1990 and 1998 (Pincus and Winters 2003: 22). Wade is critical of the developmental possibilities of TRIPS (Trade-Related Aspects of Intellectual Property Rights), TRIMs Trade-Related Investment Measures), and GATS (General Agreemet on Trade in Services) (Wade 2003; see also Picciotto 1999). Add to this the specific national protectionisms that emerge from the Europe and America (steel, cognac, the CAP etc.) and one has a very dour image of the developmental prospects of global regulation.

Embedded liberalism 'worked' because it defined a functional and reasonably coordinated relationship between national models of economic management and the global economy. In light of this, embedded neoliberalism appears to be a project facing serious difficulties. The World Bank is 'projectising' embedded neoliberalism into African states with no facilitating context that might allow states to legitimise a core set of developmentally purposive policies. This makes the persistence of neoliberalism – prevalent in development thinking and policy, as well as governance discourse and practice – all the more intriguing. The next chapter explores the nature of neoliberalism's failures in more detail, allowing subsequent chapters to understand the ways in which neoliberal practices persist.

Global social practice

So far, we have identified an emerging institutional project at the global level – one that has profoundly shaped the global political economy in ways that have pushed most parts of the world towards liberal economic policy. For Africa, this global project has been manifest especially in African states' relations with the World Bank. This section will show how this global project is based in social practice rather than epochal ideational forces or abstracted capitalist logic – although clearly both of these analytical drivers are intertwined with the way social practices emerge and change. And, at this more grand level, it is only possible (in this book at least) to identify key aspects of practice in their generalities.

It is important to start by recognising that there is a global social practice. There has emerged an interconnected institutional and discursive neoliberal project which – although far from omnipotent or perfectly unified – has become increasingly prominent over the last thirty years and can now be identified in an impressive range of international organisations.

Theorists of international political economy often speak about international regimes to identify a set of global interconnections. Perhaps the clearest example of an international regime outside of our concerns here is 'the long 1960s' in which a social-democratic developmentalist regime emerged through the UN system and the politics of Independence, say from the Bandung conference in 1955 to the first Lomé agreement in 1975. During this period, a panoply of statements, institutions, financial mechanisms, rules and coalitions were formed around the basic premiss that the 'Third World' (to use the vernacular of the time) required 'differentiated and preferential treatment' (to use the vernacular of our time) in order for all nations to develop. This period witnessed the creation of the 'Paris Club' of bilateral aid donors; the creation of the 'soft' lending arm of the World Bank, the International Development Association; the declaration of a 'development decade' by the UN; the creation of the Development Assistance Committee within the OECD, the inauguration of the Non-Aligned Movement, the creation of the UN Conference on Trade and Development, the emergence of the Group of 77 post-colonial states within the UN General Assembly, the creation of the UN Development Programme, UN Covenants on Civil and Political Rights and Social and Economic Rights, price stabilisation funds for primary commodities, and the Declaration of a New International Economic Order.

The point is not to argue a certain degree of success or failure for this regime. Rather, it is to provide an analogy with the current neoliberal international regime. And, indeed, one can identify a similar period in which international 'regimental' activities produce a constellation of institutions, discourses and practices that shift international politics away from social-democratic developmentalism towards neoliberalism – in this latter case over a longer period.

Throughout the last twenty years, a massive global alignment has taken place. The Lomé agreements between the EU and the ACP groups of post-colonial states has been determinedly liberalised since Lomé III (1983); the USA left the 'developmentalist' UNESCO in 1984, commencing an undermining of the UN organisations that grew during the previous regime; the World Bank created MIGA, which clearly sees development not through concessional lending for social and economic public projects but through the incentivisation of private capital; the GATT Uruguay Round commenced in 1986, ending of course with the creation of the WTO; price stabilisation funds were abolished or underfunded (for example, the International Coffee Agreement ended in 1989); the World Bank and the IMF developed a range of lending programmes based on 'systemic' and macroeconomic neoliberal reforms; G7 and G8 meetings became more regularised and important; NAFTA was created; the Basle 'Core Principles' of international banking were created; a Financial Stability Forum was created; World Bank, IMF, and WTO annual summits, World Economic Forums, G8 pre-summit meetings and 'green room' politics, and so on produce a networked and powerful international neoliberal 'architecture', which, by the 2000s, has produced the best evidence of social globalisation that we have.

The extent of integration between different international organisations is high and indeed difficult to map out fully precisely because of the complexity and density of interconnection – both formal and informal. Furthermore, interconnections work across and between governments, intergovernmental organisations, and private agencies such as bond rating agencies, associations of banks, accounting standards agencies and so on. We can provide a flavour here before moving on to a more reflective understanding of the nature of social practice. It is not my intention to encompass all aspects of this global neoliberal networking; rather, I wish just to provide a convincing sense of the level and intensity of interconnection.

The World Bank and the IMF have become closely intertwined since the creation of SAP. Currently, HIPC and the PRSP both require Bank–IMF co-production: each institution has related funding mechanisms (PRSC and PRGF), joint evaluation of PRSP is required, and currently PRSPs are integrated into a World Bank/IMF Integrated Framework. The World Bank and the IMF have developed a 'Coherence Agenda' since the mid-1990s. They also co-produce a Financial Sector Assessment Programme. The IMF's date generation and auditing functions connect it to the OECD (as a participant in Inter Ministerial Finance Committee Meetings). The IMF sends its confidential Country Reports to the WTO, which in turn holds joint research seminars with the IMF – and the World Bank. In 1996, the WTO, the World Bank and IMF agreed codes of cooperation, reinforced as a 'Joint Declaration of Coherence' during the 1999 WTO meeting in Seattle, and throughout the WTO Doha 'Development Round'. The WTO has observer status on the World Bank and IMF Executive Boards. The WTO has effectively claimed the 'hard' regulatory functions of international trade, leaving the UNCTAD with a residual role concerned with the social impacts of trade but little effective power since the mid-1990s. Outside of the 'unholy trinity' (Peet 2003) revolve a constellation of other agencies which rely on data and funds from the 'big three', such as the International Accounting Standards Board, the Bank of International Settlements, and the World Intellectual Property Organisation.

It is readily apparent that this neoliberal architecture is substantial and built around a laissez-faire agenda. What kind of social practice underpins this project?

5

Neoliberal practice in Africa

THIS CHAPTER is organised into three bundles, each of which identifies a salient aspect of neoliberal practice in Africa. Although cases are drawn from a wide range of country cases, the bulk of the evidence derives from those states which have undergone the most protracted and extensive neoliberal intervention.

The framing of neoliberal intervention in Africa is powerfully focused on the state (Moore 1999). This is, of course, a generic part of the neoliberal approach that applies in many parts of the world, but even if the focus on state modelling is not exceptional it is extreme in Africa. This largely comes under the rubric of governance (Harrison 2004), although the components that fall under this rubric are diverse and not entirely coherent. The focus on the state has led to a relatively weak focus on the private sector. Thus, when we come to look at practices of neoliberal intervention, we will be looking mainly at practices within the state. What happens in the 'private sector' is another matter.

The extent to which neoliberalism has been mainstreamed into African states is the extent to which existing state practices have been modified or entirely changed and new practices introduced. These modified and changed practices have been realised in a transnational social space (Callaghy et al. 2001), populated by representatives of donor governments, international finance and development organisations, high-level civil servants and technicians, some politicians, and intellectuals. Taken together, these individuals – probably only a few hundred in each country – represent an immense concentration of power within each and every African state. Furthermore, they are, as a group, highly integrated; this being one result of the nature of their social practice. Thus, it is within these practices of neoliberal execution that we find the dynamic of neoliberal intervention: not across a line of sovereignty but rather a transnational bundle of practices that has grown within the state and that aims to transform state practice – and perhaps social practice more generally – in its entirety.

The following sections give an overview of the patterns of neoliberal practice with special attention to the sequencing of reform efforts.

Conduct

Let us start with conduct as it sets a normative framing for habits and repertoire. Conduct is produced through discourse and behaviour by all of those involved in the execution of neoliberal reform. Initially, employees of international organisations and Western states established a prototype framework for neoliberal conduct. This was crude, provisional and associated with an undertow of coercion, as most African states were only engaging with international organisations and neoliberal reform as a result of severe economic crisis. This normative neoliberal kernel associated good practice with economic liberalisation. It was largely economistic and was based on an implicit norm of efficacy. To adapt Alexander Pope's bon mot, neoliberal conduct was 'whatever is best for liberalisation is best'. As a result, conduct was diffuse – that is, driven by external actions and a scattering of the converted within African governments. External agents would intervene strongly

– perhaps coercively – to pursue neoliberal reforms: meetings with government officials would be adversarial and often based on the possibility of the withdrawal of funding. Those within government who took on reform agendas might aim to execute those agendas with a view to expedience and necessity rather than any broader normative construction. Indeed, those responsible for structural adjustment programmes often felt like a small cadre of reformers working against the tide of government and society.

Examples of the practices associated with this early neoliberal conduct include the negotiation of structural adjustment credit lines in Washington (not in-country). Sometimes, the negotiations would pre-empt any parliamentary discussion of general budgeting, as happened in Mozambique (Harrison 1999a). In fact, many budgets in highly indebted countries require IMF approval before being presented to the parliament or national assembly (Hanlon and Smart 2008: 98). In 2003, the Ghanaian parliament approved new tariffs on rice and poultry imports (in order to protect domestic producers), but after meetings with the IMF and World Bank these were rescinded (Parfitt 2009: 48–9).

In some cases, the authoritarian structures of state power afforded by military rule or concentrated presidential executives facilitated 'stroke of the pen' practices in which exchange rates were liberalised, permissive investment laws introduced, marketing boards abolished, and price subsidies removed with little if any parliamentary or public discussion. In Zambia, 'it was reported that a meeting of the Cabinet and central Committee, presented with the idea of another IMF programme at short notice, voted overwhelmingly against it. This vote was overturned by the President, who was supported only by the Ministers of Finance and Agriculture' (Harvey 1991: 131).

In Mozambique, where SAP was introduced in 1987, prices had been partially liberalised previously, but in 1988 subsidies were removed from basic staple foods. As a result, the price of a kilogram of rice rose by 575 per cent, of maize by 317 per cent, of sugar by 428 per cent and that of a loaf of bread by 50 per cent, (Marshall 1990: 31). This rendered a basic subsistence way out of reach of the average wage earner (Hermele 1988). In Tanzania, where SAP was introduced in 1986 (after a series of 'home grown' attempts at adjustment), basic commodity prices followed a similar trend: from 1985 to 1988, the per kilogram price of sugar rose by 266 per cent, soap by 396 per cent, and kangas (cloth for clothing) by 920 per cent (Messkoub 1996). In Zimbabwe, during the first two years of Bank-sponsored adjustment, average earnings fell by 24 per cent in real terms (Gibbon 1996: 379). In Sierra Leone in 1986, after adjustment and devaluation, the price of a bar of soap rose fourfold from Leone 0.5 to 2, a gallon of kerosene rose from Leone 9 to Leone 23 and a chicken quadrupled from Leone 20 to Leone 80 (Riddell 1992: 57).

Many SAPs also included policies of *retrenchment* in the public sector – the largest employer in most African countries. Consequently, SAP has led to higher numbers of unemployed. In Uganda, a World Bank-supported retrenchment programme had cut the public employee list from 320,000 to 150,000 between 1990 and 1995 (Bigsten and Kayizzi-Mugerwa 1999: 64–5). In Ghana, retrenchment as part of its SAP led to the cutting of 53,000 civil servants by 1989 (Rothchild 1991: 9).

The conduct of practice was, then, largely based on implementation. Good conduct was *consequential* – that is, evaluated by its ends/outcomes, not its means. The norms of implementation were effective, quick and radical reform, or even 'shock'. There was often a sense that neoliberal reformers within African states were a vanguard: equivalents of Chile's 'Chicago boys' or Gaidar and Chubalis in Russia, who had close contacts with the World Bank and the IMF, and a 'scientific' value system in which 'politics' was an encumbrance or a set of relations to be manipulated to realise neoliberal ends (Milder 1996: 151).

This was the nature of neoliberal conduct throughout the 1980s: an emaciated set of norms which did not speak to the issues of rights, justice or even social well-being, but rather saw good politics as effective and obedient implementation of good science. There was a necessitarian kernel to conduct during this period, which was rather well and aptly summarised (unintentionally) by the UK Conservative Party's 1997 slogan 'Yes, it hurts. Yes, it works.' In other words, little thought was given to the disruption and hardship directly caused by SAP – the neoliberal model's realisation was the overwhelming priority. In fact, social 'costs' only came prominently onto the radar when they threatened implementation as a result of riots and protests; if people suffered quietly, their suffering barely registered within emerging and combative neoliberal cliques.

This state of affairs was gradually overlain by other practices, which generated 'thicker' notions of conduct. Those involved in neoliberal reforms soon found that the simple consequentialism of 'stroke-of-the-pen' changes did not necessarily have the desired effects, and certainly did not achieve a full neoliberal transition. As a result, consultants, policymakers, and representatives of the donor/creditor organisations developed more ambitious programmes which aimed to change the nature and remit of state action and also to implement social policy. Examples of these programmes include: the creation of social 'safety nets' for those considered to be transiently damaged by marketisation; the creation of new state institutions to monitor and manage resources more efficiently; a range of education/socialisation programmes aimed at state employees and also social groups more broadly; and capacity-building projects to shore up the rule of law and property rights.

The development of neoliberal social policy – essentially to offset the transition costs of liberalisation – only created a slender modification of existing neoliberal conduct. This new managerialism – in which social provision is rendered as 'effective, efficient and economic management of human and capital resources' (Yeatman 1990: 40) – was grafted on to existing forms of administrative conduct: a self-standing 'safety net' to ensure that neoliberal objectives were achieved. Seen in this light, social safety nets were part of neoliberal science; a modification to a model to ensure its viability. As such, these programmes did little to push forward broader changes in conduct. The provision of vouchers, means-tested social support, and ring-fenced money for basic health and education fitted well within existing neoliberal practices. It required neither a deepening of neoliberal conduct into a more normatively rich practice, nor a broader expansion of neoliberal practice beyond the international agencies and the nodes of reform that they had generated within the apex of the state.

In the mid-1980s, the *dirigiste* liberalisation of SAP was expanded to include aspects of social amelioration. SAPs became ESAPS (economic and social structural adjustment programmes). The best-known example of this shift was PAMSCAD (Programme for the Amelioration of the Social Costs of Adjustment) in Ghana (Hutchful 1994; Zack-Williams 2000). Mozambique undertook PRES in 1987 (Programa de Reforma Económica e Social), Zimbabwe introduced an ESAP in 1991, and so on. These programmes contained measures such as a Social Development Fund 'designed to minimise the effects of austerity on vulnerable groups' (Government of Zimbabwe, cited in Logan and Tevera 2001: 110). These programmes have a common logic, which is encapsulated fairly transparently in the unwieldy acronym PAMSCAD; as such, they recognised that neoliberal reforms required a certain kind of 'social sensitivity' which was absent during the early 1980s with its conduct of determined necessity. But these programmes did not seek to do anything more than ease difficult neoliberal transitions (Saunders 1996); as such, they were designed to provide transitory 'safety nets' for those who were contingently losing out during the shift to a neoliberal political economy. As such, the conduct of implementation here was *managerial*, not social-democratic: the rolling out of social components generated a stronger conduct within states concerned not solely with liberalisation but also with public management. 'Good' reform increasingly came to involve a broader understanding of development management which required an awareness of social suffering and the potential this might have for social disruption or protest. Neoliberal conduct thus became more complex in its normative framing – and not entirely coherent. There existed within many states a constant tension between bold reform and the management of the effects of these reforms. As a result, neoliberal cadres (national and international) began to speak increasingly of the importance of well-designed reform scheduling. Indeed, reform came to be valued not simply for its determined necessity but also for its nuance in balancing liberalisation with social peace and state stability.

Conduct was fashioned out of this incremental and iterated expansion of the policy remit of neoliberal programmes. Those within the international organisations wished not only to expand the remit of neoliberal intervention, but also to develop mechanisms to enhance the predictability of increasingly 'involved' reforms. The lodestone here was a concern with corruption and a corresponding construction of good conduct based in transparency (Brown and Cloke 2004). As many bilateral aid budgets grew in the West during the 1990s, Western governments also supported an increasingly prominent advocacy of 'good governance', which had at its heart a formulation of good conduct based in transparency and accountability. African policymakers and administrators engaged with the discourse of good governance, co-authoring the good practice discourse against corruption and promoting transparency, honesty and efficiency.

In 1994, the World Bank gave its clearest generic definition of governance reform as the promotion of a more efficient public administration, the promotion of accountability, the establishment of the rule of law and a capable judiciary, and transparency (World Bank 1994b: ch. 1). Within these broad programmatic indicators, policies emerged that once again expanded the nature of neoliberalism, marking a decidedly strong focus on re-engineering the state.

In his analysis of Tanzania, Mozambique and Uganda, Harrison identifies a raft of policies that have served to realise governance: administrative reform, new information management systems, incentivisation within the state, new financial management systems, the creation of new agencies to promote transparency, new modes of policymaking which include other 'stakeholders' (Harrison 2005).

It was this increasing intertwining of internal and external agents and their developing of a more explicitly normative discourse concerning conduct that led to the nebulous discursive constructions of neoliberal propriety that we can see today in many states. Anti-corruption discourse remains prominent, accompanied by statements, training programmes and information management systems which aim to engineer efficient and accountable public servants. Anti-corruption reform practice involved a number of changes to conduct. First, the internal auditing and financial management systems of states were bolstered, but this also led to a deeper process of invigilation in which surveillance cascaded throughout the institutions of government. This is set out in the Tanzanian Public Sector Reform programme for example (Harrison 2004). The 'islands of integrity' approach to corruption (Klitgaard 1988) was replaced by more encompassing attempts to change the habits of governance (Williams 1996). Public officials were also expected to change their practices of service delivery: away from the hierarchical structures of the 'office holder' faced with a citizen or subject towards the consumerist ethos of a service provider engaging with a client or customer. Complaints processes were publicised, posters setting out clients' rights were placed on public office walls, and deadlines for the completion of requests made of public officials were set out and publicised.

These kinds of reforms were devised by policymakers, always with technical assistance and advice from international consultants and experts, to impose stronger codes of conduct (sometimes literally so-called) on the public administration as a whole. This was a practice of mainstreaming transparent, efficient and disciplined modes of work throughout states. The success that this endeavour enjoyed is another matter, as we shall see in Chapter 6.

Decentralisation programmes aim to produce accountable public servants – accountable not to the monitoring eyes of superiors but to the citizenry of the local administrative boundaries. We shall return to this in more detail in the next chapter. Ideals of political will and leadership have become more foregrounded. The last norm mentioned above – political will/leadership – deserves separate comment. This norm is not practised solely in its discursive production, but is also integrated into significant changes in the way neoliberal reform is governed. This is manifested in the expression of a desire to put countries 'in the driving seat' of neoliberal reform, or, more programmatically, to generate 'ownership' of reforms by locating various aspects of policymaking within African states. The best example of this is the Poverty Reduction Strategy Paper, which has integrated into it the 'process conditionality' that in-country consultation precedes the writing of a PRSP by the lending government. We will return to this innovation in the policy process in the next section.

In sum, neoliberal conduct has been produced through the increasingly integrated discursive and programmatic constructions within the transnational social space outlined above. 'Good conduct' has moved from a bare consequentialism to a more normatively rich ideal-type of a certain kind of self who is motivated, efficient, transparent and accountable in ways that personify the ideal of a market agent. The conduct of African officials has become increasingly foregrounded as a result of the emphasis on ownership. Ownership has been created by the affirmation of practices of leadership and consultation within African governments.

Habit

The habits of neoliberal practice did not develop in a stable incremental fashion. Neoliberalism began as an external intervention to liberalise; thus in most states neoliberal practices were new and often starkly different to existing habits of governance (van de Walle 2001). They were largely seen as discrete acts rather than as part of existing routines and institutions. The context of pervasive political instability that existed through the 1980s also stymied the development of neoliberal habits in many cases. Neoliberal practices were developed in environments of unstable elections, protest, and economic instability and recession (see Chapter 2), rendering it extremely difficult to make neoliberalism routine practice. Policies might be reversed, ignored or undermined under the pressures of regime change, security demands or the acts of elites whose main aim was/is to ensure their survival and, if possible, their enrichment. Nevertheless, since the early 1990s there has emerged a bundle of habits of neoliberal governance. These habits are interpolated with the deepening norms of neoliberal conduct outlined above; they are the practices that routinise notions of efficiency, transparency, reform leadership and so on. We can identify some key characteristics of this routinisation of neoliberal practice: 'new' governance, depoliticisation and sociability.

'New' governance

For many states, the shift from the halting discrete acts of neoliberal reform to a more incremental and habitual neoliberal practice was underpinned by the construction of a sense of political transition. This sense of a changing political scene was not marked by the election of new parties to power: as we discussed in Chapter 2, multiparty politics was shaped in ways that largely conformed to neoliberal coordinates in that commonly contesting parties did not bring alternative development agendas into the public sphere; in fact, if anything, they pretended that they would make better custodians of the neoliberal social engineering project. Rather, the sense of change derived from shifts within existing party-states, underpinning the importance of political stability to the consolidation of neoliberal habits. In Tanzania, this was marked by the succession of President Ali Hassan Mwinyi by Benjamin Mkapa (and continues under Mkapa's successor Jakaya Kikwete). In Ghana and Uganda the shift was marked by a determined reconciliation of the president with the World Bank and the IMF after short periods of inchoate economic populism. In Malawi, the shift was marked by a party shift from the Malawi Congress Party to the United Democratic Front, as it was in Zambia – a country particularly hit by stand-offs with the IMF – from the United National Independence Party to the Movement for Multiparty Democracy. In other countries, reconciliation with the World Bank and the IMF after countries had been declared 'off track' had much of their lending frozen served to establish this sense of newness. In other cases, new regimes that came to power through military victory were seen as offering a 'fresh start': this was seen as the case in Ethiopia, (after a short interlude) Uganda, and Rwanda (Ottaway 1996).

In each of these cases, ruling elites and much of the 'international community' constructed a sense of *tabula rasa* (with the signal exception of considering debt run up by previous regimes as illegitimate) in which neoliberal practice might be introduced more ambitiously within new political contexts. This political 'window' allowed for a mainstreaming of neoliberal reforms as ruling elites made significant changes to the institutions of governance and propounded ideologies of rule based in newness: recovery, sweeping government clean, and new orders provided the political metaphors for this shift.

Depoliticisation

It is in the essence of habit that the political content of practice tends to be obscured. Observers have noted how neoliberal development has been increasingly formulated in depoliticised ways: as apolitical, as a concern with proper (scientific) technique, or as common sense. But how has this emerged through governance practice?

The ways in which this depoliticisation came about refer us to a bundle of practices that were consolidated throughout the 1990s. Policymaking and evaluation became increasingly shaped by international discourses of development technique. International aid and lending organisations have funded analyses by consultants and the location of expatriate technical assistance within African states in order to develop 'parametric' management systems, in other words the general frameworks within which recourse allocation, information management, human resource management and institutional development take place. This has involved a substantial 'computerisation' of institutions, along with the introduction of software packages for record-keeping, financial management and so on. The logical framework has been introduced as the 'parametric' frame for policy implementation and evaluation: schedules of expenditure, and outputs within time-specific matrices. As a result of training programmes, and the funding of bright new technicians in courses and degrees in Europe and the USA, these parameters of governance have been increasingly rolled out into bureaucracies and become part of the day-to-day practice of resource and information management.

These ways of governing have all been articulated as techniques, not political devices. They are seen as value-neutral or scientific. They have enabled a series of routinised practices: data generation for new forms of state management, new ways of managing expenditures, meetings to discuss outputs and inputs into administrative systems, and so on. The infusion of governmental institutions with imperatives of efficiency, incentivisation and budgetary austerity has been consolidated through ostensibly apolitical 'best international practice'.

Sociability

There are many examples of specific sites where habits have emerged: the various sectoral working groups which meet every month or so to consider reform progress and prospects; the inter-ministerial technical committees which are staffed by high-level bureaucrats and economists; the consultation mechanisms that have emerged with the mainstreaming of PRSP (SAPRIN 2004); the general profusion of workshops in which civil servants, academics, various experts and donor officials congregate to reflect on topics such as corruption, pro-poor growth or decentralisation (Green 2003; Holtom 2005); the entertaining of a raft of 'missions' arriving from the headquarters of international organisations and bilateral governments. All of these have produced what Whitfield calls 'institutional memory' (2005: 652), forged out of the routinised practices of neoliberal governance.

It is within these forums – and others more or less country-specific and formal – that habitual practices of neoliberal governance have emerged. Those involved in these institutions have innovated languages, images, networks, knowledges, norms and patterns of mobility which produce neoliberal governance within states. Once again, it is noteworthy that this is a transnational domain; that is, one in which both African national and expatriate personnel of various kinds intermingle.

Repertoire

So far, we have sketched how neoliberal practices have generated a set of norms and habits that have consolidated themselves within a transnational group within states from the early 1990s. This section recognises that these routines and norms have been not only embodied in practices, but also strongly shaped by the sense of possibility created by the context within which neoliberalism has expanded throughout African states. Most obviously, neoliberalism is premissed on the high level of economic vulnerability of African states which leaves them with high levels of external debt, a high dependence on aid and credit, and fragile economies. The possibilities for practices of governance in many states are shaped by material dependence on international donors and creditors. This is not to say that practice is narrowly determined by the material predominance of external agencies; there are always diversities in social practice because all practices involve some creativity by the actor (Bhabha 2004). But the ways in which practices emerge and the nature of the choice between different practices are nevertheless strongly conditioned by issues relating to funding, credit, aid bargaining and the attraction of foreign investment. Some options are rendered less attractive than others because of the ways in which funding possibilities are structured; some options evoke likely ruptures in the general material disposition between a state and the donor groupings which would introduce radical uncertainty and a shift away from pre-existing habits and conducts.

Thus, here we are concerned to sketch the neoliberal repertoire – the ways in which practices have reconciled themselves to the fact that many African states are materially fragile and international donor/credits groups are a major source of funds for a wide range of developmental activities. This reconciliation of practice with a neoliberal repertoire also reinforces the latter – it is not simply practice conforming to an externally funded model but also a repertoire that gains its strength as social practice, which gives it greater prominence than it would have simply through control over the purse strings.

It is easy enough to recognise the basic repertoire of neoliberalism. It derives from the ways in which perceived serious deviation from the neoliberal model evoked the freezing of credit tranches, potential IMF declarations that a country had gone 'off track', or even the rescinding of lines of credit. As we have seen, this politics of adherence and delinquency accompanied the first decade of neoliberalism, broadly mapping onto the rudimentary neoliberal conduct outlined in the first section of this chapter. Neoliberal repertoires in this period were as likely to produce adversarial practices as conforming ones. Adherence to a project might have involved nothing more than a minimal conformity in order to assure that external resources flowed.

But, as habits and conduct have deepened, the neoliberal repertoire has become more embedded in social practice. Access to aid
and credit has infused itself deeply into the workings of governance.
Aid technicians and high-level civil servants have articulated the
language of international development into their own policymaking
and discussions with external agency representatives: mainstreaming, output orientation, participation, expenditure tracking, the
language of clients and customers, and so on. Each of these tropes
is based on a bolder formulation of neoliberal 'roll out' in which the
'hard' liberalisation and state rollback is expanded (not replaced)
by a more ambitious project of state and even social engineering.
Whatever the merits of this language, or aspects of it, the practising
of this kind of development discourse both conforms to international development norms and works to assure or attract further
tranches of external funding embedded in ongoing development
policy and programmes.

One can see this clearly in the ways in which the PRSP has
produced a repertoire of social practice within African states.
PRSPs, which are designed to be created by African governments
with some form of civil society participation, have produced a familiar neoliberal template across Africa (Stewart and Wang 2003).
It would appear that those technicians who design the PRSP
understand very well the importance of an 'appealing' PRSP that
speaks to donors and creditors who have three-year plans for their
bilateral aid budgets, Comprehensive Development Frameworks,
and Poverty Reduction Growth Facilities to disburse. In this
context, practices of pre-emptive conformity emerge. Therkildsen
find this in Tanzania (2000); and Fraser speaks of a 'cut and paste'
aspect to Ghana's PRSP (2005: 656; see also Whitfield 2005).

The point of this section is not to comment on the motivations of
officials, but rather to note how neoliberal practice has generated a
repertoire of governance based on languages and techniques which
serve in some way to reinforce conduits of external resources and
the continued positive engagement of external agencies. A material

dependency that evoked sensibilities of sovereignty throughout the 1980s has created new practices which have accepted the preponderance of external agencies, and subsequently consolidated robust boundaries around the politics of the possible.

Neoliberalism in action: public-sector reform

In Bank project documentation, central attention is paid to the adoption and 'rolling out' of new procedural protocols. It is here that we find all of the assumptions of New Public Management in the Bank's praxis. The key processes are Results Oriented Management (ROM), Performance Improvement Modelling (PIM), and Output Oriented Budgeting (OOB). ROM aims to replace a supposedly entrenched protocol of resource management based on inputs. Most strongly in Tanzania, budgets were previously set by the ministry of finance on the basis of perceived necessary inputs to a ministry, department or agency, with little regard to the efficiency of resource use or the pressures that this form of indicative spending put on the budget. ROM aims to tie resource use to the measurement of results achieved in an executing agency. This is to be achieved through the introduction of strategic planning and latterly OOB, in which budgets are revised upwards or downwards in relation to the achievement of a series of discrete and measurable outputs. Technically, the introduction of ROM and OOB has proved very challenging, especially in Uganda. But these techniques render public administration akin to a series of quasi-independent and firm-like bodies, in which revenue (largely funding envelopes from the ministry of finance) depend on sales or services rendered (outputs of a specific agency). Closely associated with these reforms, both Uganda's and Tanzania's ministries of finance have made considerable efforts to introduce more flexible, centralised and austere forms of budgetary management, again with Bank and other donors' funding and technical assistance. The key reform here is the Medium Term Expenditure Framework, which both countries are implementing. This has, in the first place, made it more difficult for specific ministries to gain discretionary funding through special pleading and has opened up the possibility of ministries of finance rewarding efficient departments with extra funds from one quarter to another.

Thus, one can identify a raft of integrated techniques, prominently dealt with in Bank programme documentation, focused on the creation of NPM-like internal structures of public administration. The conceptualisation of agency within this scheme is intended to ensure purposeful and competent principals at different nodes in the reform process. For example, the Tanzania Accountability Transparency and Integrity Project (2001) is based on a 'commitment of political leaders' to the reforms (World Bank 2000b: 2) and another project relies on a 'cadre of senior public service mangers with skills' (World Bank 2004b: 4). This reflects a general desire by the Bank to ensure that the projects it funds have 'champions' or 'change agents' within the bureaucracy. These individuals are the ones who receive requisite training (at higher levels training in the West) and who are expected to prosecute reforms throughout the state. They are usually permanent secretaries, directors or executive agents of departments and agencies. But the Bank does not rely entirely on reform-friendly principals; the broader ontology of agency is that all public employees (agents) will become 'incentivised' to embrace NPM-like changes to their work. This is the logic behind the Performance Improvement Models which are the foundation of Tanzania's Bank-funded Public Sector Reform Programme. The model works broadly as follows: employees agree with the nearest superior a set of targets to achieve and to be reviewed periodically (Adam and Gunning 2002). The longer-term aim is to integrate these with pay-scale reform. Pay scales in both countries have been under pressure from the Bank and other donors to 'decompress' – that is, to create larger increments for those who achieve (technically derived and meritocratic) promotion.

The enhancement of incentives within public administration provides the 'carrot' to accompany the 'stick' of increased invigilation. The latter is one way in which the broad reference to transparency is concretised in governance reform. Information management has received funding from a variety of donors, including the World Bank, and there are three key processes that are noteworthy and have had real effects on administration. First, payroll reform (one of the first reform initiatives in both Tanzania's and Uganda's civil-service reform) has made employment within the civil service more transparent, introducing new procedures for payment that eradicate 'ghost' workers and monetising perquisites such as free housing or a car and driver. Second, invigorated procedures of monitoring and evaluation have been part of both countries' administrative reform programmes. Third, new budgetary techniques have forced ministries, departments and agencies to report financial management in more detail to the ministry of finance. This is a central aspect of the introduction of Medium Term Expenditure Frameworks in both countries (supported by Bank macroeconomic lending and/or budget support: World Bank 1999) and the introduction of public expenditure reviews which can track resource use down the hierarchy of agencies and produce very detailed information (Reinikka and Collier 2001). Thus, the public employee, as a rational maximising individual, has a radically modified incentive structure in which both the gains to hard work and the losses of poor work are increased; furthermore, the risks of being caught misusing resources are greater.

The introduction of new public management reforms, based on assumptions concerning rational choice and principals and agents, represents a radical departure from the administrative logics that previously existed within Uganda's and Tanzania's bureaucracies (Langseth and Mugaju 1996). Furthermore, the reforms have been introduced into emaciated administrations – poorly resourced or, in Uganda's case, all but entirely depleted by a long period of civil war and extreme authoritarianism. As a result, governance reforms have been as concerned with *constructing* the state as they have with *reforming* it. Furthermore, as these states have received substantial amounts of aid and loans, they have become the premier actor in promoting market-based economic growth. As Mosley argues, using aid and loans to promote the institutional development of the state is key to the promotion of economic growth and development (Mosley 2004). Thus, capacity-building programmes – both self-standing and as components of other programmes – serve the dual purpose of enabling states to internalise new administration logics and constructing state infrastructure from the denuded foundations left from previous periods. For example, the Bank-funded Institutional Capacity Building Project sets out a remit which overlaps considerably with the Civil Service Reform Programme in that it focuses heavily on public administration, and sets out a broad range of training packages – at a cost of $25 milliion – which the Bank judged largely to be successful (World Bank 1995b, 2000a).

The place of neoliberal practice in African states and societies

The previous sections have outlined neoliberalism's progress not as a generic idea or imperative, but as the development of bundles of conduct, habit and repertoire which collectively provide us with a sense of how social practices within African states have *produced* neoliberalism. Neoliberal practice, we have seen, can be identified in discourse, techniques of development management, and institutions that have consolidated themselves within a transnational social space. Neoliberal practice is how neoliberalism is executed in specific national instantiation; it is the embodiment of neoliberalism in the conduct of people as they reflect on the possibilities of action, the constraints they face and the dispensations of power that they find themselves in.

Our approach thus far reveals a striking contrast. Considered as a global generic idea, neoliberalism suggests a bold project of social engineering – a tsunami to borrow Ong's figurative representation (2007a; see also Harvey 2007: 23). Even if neoliberalism is 'dirty' and complex on the ground, there is often a sense of a global 'great transformation' or global constitutionalism (Gill 1995). But, on the other hand, neoliberal practice in Africa has been incremental and 'cloistered'. That is, it has not created marketised *tabulae rasae* so much as emerged out of existing socialities; and this emergence has been substantially limited to a transnational elite within the apexes of the state. Even in those states that have commonly been perceived as 'champions' of neoliberal reform – Ghana, Uganda, Tanzania, Mozambique, and perhaps others such as Zambia, Burkina Faso, Malawi – are often plagued by the expression of doubts as to how extensive or consolidated reforms are. Furthermore, this analysis has not looked at other practices within African states, which still encompass substantial habits constructed on patronage, clientelism and ethnic considerations. This is before we consider the impact of neoliberalism on African markets, which most current research suggests are infused with non-neoliberal habits, conduct and repertoire – even as they produce new forms of accumulation and enrichment (Cramer et al. 2008).

At this point, it is instructive to return to a more general frame of reference. If we accept that neoliberal habits are 'in construction' and largely delimited to the central state, and that outside of this bundle of practices there is every reason to expect to find varied forms of social practice, we see that Africa is no different to any other region or country. Even the most reified neoliberal projects pursued extremely aggressively in 'developed' capitalist economies have not rendered societies in their own image. Prominent examples such as the USA, the UK and New Zealand all in their own way show how nationalism, patronage, public moralities, social resistance, emerge out of non-neoliberal practices, which means that it would be wrong to speak of neoliberal societies or even to assume an *a priori* direction to the ways in which these societies will change.

This seems to be at the heart of neoliberal social engineering. Neoliberalism as practice is not simply imposed by the North on the South; nor is it a form of capitalist imperialism, because capitalist social relations are not straightforwardly neoliberal. Neoliberalism can be understood to codify in ideological terms an important framework to regulate accumulation and class relations but it would be historically naive to assume a homology between neoliberal and capitalism. Rather, neoliberal intervention has emerged as a practice in many places throughout the world, giving it an image of universality, but it has not achieved anything more than an *ambition* – a sense of its own limits and an impatience with these. It is this sense that energises new practices of intervention, not simply across state borders or between North and South but within more complex geographies within and between states and societies. Neoliberal intervention within a pragmatist framework does not suggest that we are in a post-neoliberal age but rather that the significance of intervention can be found in the ways neoliberal habits, conduct and repertoire intervene in other realms of practice.

6

Neoliberalism's final frontier?

THE LAST two chapters have looked at neoliberal practice at two levels but also in two different ways. Chapter 4 focused on the construction of a global neoliberal regime and highlighted the importance of the institutionalisation (mainly through the World Bank) of this regime. This regime serves as the formative context for interventions in states – not just by the World Bank but by a broader set of international organisations. It was this intervention in African states was the that concern of Chapter 5. There we saw how neoliberal practice – conduct, habit, and repertoire – had emerged in African states. We highlighted how neoliberal practice has persisted, and after some time expanded throughout African states. We have seen this in the deepening political/normative conduct, more consolidated habits, and a reconciliation of governmental practice with the repertoire of options set out by global neoliberal institutions and, more specifically, the economic dependence of African states on aid and credit.

But so far we have been looking at a quite limited social space. For all of the changes that have happened in global and governmental practice – the liberalisation and colonisation of public action by market or market-like practices – we have not stepped out of a

transnational space inhabited by the representatives of multilateral
and bilateral credit/aid agencies, consultants, high-ranking civil
servants, postgraduate economists within state institutions, some
ministers, and a few think-tanks and civil society organisations.
This chapter investigates the extent and modalities of the diffusion
of neoliberal practice beyond this realm of neoliberal practice.

The world-view expressed by neoliberal theorists is based on
a holistic vision in which all aspects of social life (within the
state, the market, cultural relations and the family) are rendered
akin to the free-market model. But, as we have seen, neoliberal
practices have been constituted in a highly centralised and statist
fashion with little consideration as to how reforms might impact
upon the complex and diverse societies that collectively make up
most post-colonial African nations. This chapter is interested in
the fortunes of neoliberalism in Africa in terms of its realisation
in practices that potentially have an impact throughout a country,
encompassing a diversity of localities within a national space.

Vectors of neoliberal governance reform

Top-down

As we saw in Chapter 5, one of the main programmes to realise
governance reform has been the public sector reform. PSR has
attracted considerable amounts of external credit, grants and technical assistance (Harrison 2005). The World Bank is often the lead
donor with public sector reform – dedicating about one-sixth of
its project funding to PSR in 2006, representing a doubling since
1999 (*Bretton Woods Update* 61: 7). These external resources have
gone a long way to producing programmes that have as their overall
aim a wide-ranging reconstruction of the state.

This reconstruction is based on a range of assumed potential
complementarities between the state and society. In particular,
if neoliberal reformers can 'get the institutions right', then the
state will come to enable the emergence of societies that resemble

the liberal ideal-type: government accountable to citizens; individualised, competitive and largely socially harmonious societies cleaving to the basic laws of a legitimate state. And yet policy documents for neoliberal reform programmes give little clue as to how the programme might be 'rolled out' or 'embedded' within society. This is highly significant. Consider the forms of practice in Chapter 5: neoliberal practices have emerged most strikingly and strongly within a specific arrangement of conduct, habit and repertoire that only exists within a 'realm of neoliberal practice'. In Chapter 3, we saw how pragmatist approaches perceived practice as reflexive and political; in this view, there is no good reason to suppose that neoliberal practice will 'naturally' or automatically emerge once the apex of the state has set out its PRSP.

When interviewing government and donor personnel in Uganda and Tanzania, it became clear that governance reform was in essence a discourse produced by a restricted group of people which had attained a significant degree of 'enclosure' – a 'pocket' of ownership (cf. Evans and Ngalwea 2003); a realm of neoliberal practice underpinned by resource inputs and new intellectual fashions.

This 'realm' does not sit well with the broader normative thrust of the governance agenda, which has become increasingly 'inclusive' and expansive (Porter and Craig 2004), relying on terms such as stakeholding, participation and accountability. The implication of neoliberal social engineering, indeed its normative core, is that a *sine qua non* of its effective realisation is a broad civic constituency of support (Williams 1999). If elites matter, it is only inasmuch as they engage with, mobilise or create broader liberal bases of support for reform. Within its own terms, it is an oxymoron to speak of top-down neoliberal reform.

So, how do we make sense of the fact that neoliberal practice has been 'cloistered' for such an extended period? Perhaps one of the most fruitful approaches to take here emerges from development ethnography/critical anthropology, which looks centrally at development practice. A good example of this is Maia Green's study of project management in Tanzania, in which the workshop constitutes the cradle for a 'manageable' development practice that does not rely on profound considerations of success or failure but rather on the *facility* of ongoing practices and especially their conformity to global standardised models. Interestingly, she refers specifically to the LGRP (Local Government Reform Programme): 'Financed largely by multilateral and bilateral donors and designed by international audit consultancy, [it] essentially comprises a series of workshops through which local authorities are expected not merely to reform themselves, but to attain appropriate levels of competency for programme implementation' (Green 2003: 134). Interpreting Green, this is all about the employment of auditing and funding to set a repertoire for the emergence of habits that conform to international criteria of good conduct. More generally, in the work on David Mosse and others, ethnographies of professional development communities reveal how strongly influential issues of management and process are to the construction of acceptable understandings of development practice (Mosse 2005; Mosse and Lewis 2005) rather than the attainment of 'results', however defined. Uma Kothari describes how the profession of development practitioner has constructed a way of seeing and processing knowledge, and generally 'ordering' development in ways which leave little space for 'outsiders' to influence development reform (Kothari 2005). What this approach does is highlight how orthodox issues of policy success, learning and implementation are constitutive of the maintenance of a realm of neoliberal practice in which procedures and languages are maintained within an integrated and introspective (transnational) development community. These writers suggest that – as with any development policy or programme – neoliberal reform has, in a sense, taken on its own intrinsic impetus. Practices of reform become their own *raison d'être*. Its impacts outside of its own social and cognitive horizons might not be entirely disregarded, but they are not pivotal. In fact, perceived project failure might smoothly trigger commonly accepted procedures of review which integrate very easily into the existing discourse and practice.

This approach is attractive because it engages with a remarkable social development that has taken place in states like Tanzania, in which government elites which are highly dependent on external sources of revenue develop close relationships with a range of donors and creditors, in the process ostensibly internalising a very powerful global ideology of development policy. By highlighting the self-referential nature of this construction, our attention is drawn to the issue of what neoliberalism means for Tanzanian citizens in their specific localities in their encounters with the state, and how the state is changing at the local level as governance reform is 'rolled out' through decentralisation.

Bottom-up

There is a clear intellectual tradition of neoliberal theory and research which assigns a certain kind of populism to neoliberal reform (Brass 1997) based in the 'core neoclassical assumptions that markets develop naturally; that a healthy economy depends on the ability of individual economic actors to pursue their self-interests; that competition among private actors is the source of economic innovation and growth; and that excessive government intervention undermines efficient market activity' (Campbell 2001: 171; see also Peet 2002: 64). In this view, poverty is an 'accidental consequence of misfortune, unrelated to the privilege of others in the context of a ... capitalist economy' (Bracking 2004: 892). In Chapter 1 we considered how neoliberal theory understood agency through methodological individualism and rational choice; and in Chapter 5 we saw how rational-choice ideas infused practice quite centrally within PSR. There is also a more broad research agenda that shapes these quite technical and instrumental ideas of the individual into something more ambitious and socially focused. Perhaps the best place to start is with Hernando de

Soto's *The Mystery of Capital* (2001). De Soto argues that the mass poor in many parts of the world are not as asset-poor as is generally imagined. Rather, the crucial problem that produces consistent poverty is the insecurity of property. De Soto argues for a sweeping process of the securing and contractualisation of property rights and assets. This would lead to an efflorescence in poor people's (collateralised) entrepreneurialism, and as a result a profound process of poverty reduction would develop. This is not the place to review de Soto's book, which is in some respects persuasive and in others problematic, but rather to note a specific ontology embedded in the book: that the mass poor are essentially acquisitive individuals who require above all else the basic Lockean right to property in order to generate dynamic grassroots markets. The same message is provided – less elegantly – in the World Bank's *World Development Report 2000/2001*; and in *Moving Out of Poverty* (2009), which is based in the key concepts of 'initiative' and opportunity (Narayan et al. 2009: 45). Each of these major pieces of work portray societies as incipiently neoliberal: made up of individuals who want more and better market interaction, who wish to plan for an accumulation of assets, and who wish to conform to the rules of competitive market relations.

It is this context that makes the recent donor commitment to local government reform (LGR) interesting. Unlike the other main axes of neoliberal reform – financial management, civil-service reform, parliamentary reform/capacity building, data management and so on – LGR brings questions concerning neoliberal practice closer to the 'local level'; that is, to specific social contexts. LGR requires that reform-makers and implementers necessarily have to imagine how the state will act and interact with societies. In this context, 'local' simply refers to interactions outside of the governance realm and as such is a political construct that betrays the centralised nature of much reform practice. It might be more accurate to portray realms of neoliberal practice as 'local', or, perhaps better, provincial in the sense that these realms – scattered throughout African cities – are rather small and at best partially connected to the engines of African social life.

And so it is within the emerging literature on LGR and governance that we see more explicit formulations of the state–citizen interface and local state politics, beginning to construct clearer expectations of neoliberal social practice as a widespread and socially embedded phenomenon. The key premiss behind LGR is that, by localising governance reforms, citizens will identify with the former's purposes and consequently contribute to the progressive transformation of the local state. In a phrase: 'subnational governments are said to be closer to the people, have good access to local information and understand the local context well' (Smoke 2003: 9). The phrase 'bringing government closer to the people' is an oft-spoken/written one in World Bank and government documents (Barkan et al. 2004).

Tanzania presents us with a country case study in which a range of governance reforms have been pursued with strong donor backing and a relatively high degree of central government support (Harrison and Mulley 2009). This is especially the case from 1995 onwards, when donors and key parts of the government elite recognised that a disposition had been attained within which donors and the GOT had constructed a common reform agenda (Helleiner et al. 1995; Helleiner 1999; see also Chapter 5). Since the mid-1990s, the government of Tanzania has implemented new systems of transparency (financial management, data management, expenditure tracking), public-sector management (Public Sector Reform Programme, PSRP – not to be confused with the PRSP!), participation by the private sector (privatisation and contracting out), and new codes and procedures related to good governance (Ethics Secretariat, Codes of Ethics, Prevention of Corruption Bureau). Additionally, as part of the Poverty Reduction Strategy Paper (PRSP) process, Tanzania has undertaken two rounds of consultation with Tanzanian 'stakeholders' regarding general policy development. All of these reforms have contributed to the prosecution of the governance agenda at the central level, implemented upon a backdrop of (relative) political stability (with most civil unrest located in Zanzibar) with prominent high-level support, making Tanzania a 'good reformer' in most international perceptions.

Tanzania has indeed made a remarkable political journey over the last decade. It is now on its second PRSP (created in 2005 and known by its kiSwahili acronym MKUKUTA). As a result, Tanzania is intensively researched, and the downtown areas of Dar es Salaam are busy with consultants, researchers and donors. The profusion of programmes, the infusion of donor money, and the hubris of meetings, workshops and social networks represent the extent to which neoliberal practice has developed in Dar es Salaam. Interviews in 2000 and 2001 revealed that the perceived success of Tanzania's neoliberal governance reforms was intimately intertwined with the construction of a quite closed and integrated governance realm in which a certain kind of discourse – underpinned by substantial flows of resources – allowed for a high degree of 'self-referentiality' within what Gould aptly describes as a 'transnational aid domain' (Gould 2005: 63; Gould and Ojanen 2003). By this latter term, Gould means that programmes each employed similar terms as objectives and justifications, and that specific policies were articulated through similar procedures, especially logical frameworks and SWOTs (strengths, weaknesses, opportunities, threats; a similar schema is used in World Bank Project Implementation Documents).

Let us move on by looking a little further at PSR with reference to Tanzania – our case study and a country that has taken on local government reform. There are four processes encapsulated by LGR.

1. By making local government more open and transparent, local authorities and their decisions will become more legitimate.
2. As a result of the above, local groups will be more likely to support local government.

3. By devolving power to the local level, local societies will feel more disposed to engage positively with the state.

4. As a result of the above, local government will be subjected to check and balances emanating from local interest groups and organisations, making it more accountable.

It is largely through LGR that we can tease out the kinds of expectations that advocates of neoliberal reform have in regard to the latter's prospects outside of the neoliberal realm of practice occupied by donors, workshops and air conditioners. It brings our focus centrally on to the ways that reform relates to social relations outside the realm of donor and high state officials.

Diffusing neoliberal practice? LGR in Lushoto

Lushoto is located in Tanga region, a day's travel from Dar es Salaam. Although not an especially remote district compared with those in the centre and south of the country, Lushoto raises issues that are common to the districts more generally: concerns about (perceived) remoteness, a desire by some to tap into resources that are retained at the centre, a desire by the young to migrate out to the regional capital or to Dar es Salaam, and a fluid sense of Lushoto's intrinsic identity within a broader nation (Feierman 1974, 1990, 2005). Any generic policy innovation such as LGR which aims at 'the local' must necessarily negotiate the relationship between the central state and the districts, or, as I have formulated it, between the realm of neoliberal practice and specific social contexts.

LGR – like all large programmatic initiatives in indebted African states – has required funding from the World Bank and aligned international agencies. The World Bank has made decentralisation a key reform for East Africa. Following a broadly similar strategy to that pursued for central government reform, the World Bank sees the reconfiguration of local government as requiring an influx

of finance to drive reforms. As such, large amounts of money
need to be managed by the local administration (for example,
the primary and secondary education projects). A key objective
of LGR is that new planning and financial practices integrate
with previously established national ones: for example, District
Development Plans integrated into Medium Term Expenditure
Frameworks via the Integrated Financial Management System,
and the introduction of Planrep, a new planning and reporting
tool (Mushi and Melyoki n.d.: 1). Also, and relatedly, new in-
frastructures in information generation and management need to
be created; for example, preparations for the Platinum/Epicor
software system and the small projects of Rapid Rural Appraisal.
An Annual Performance Assessment System was rolled out in the
districts during 2006.

It is not possible to estimate the extent to which the LGR has
led to an increase in resource allocation to the district because the
flows to the district level are extremely complex, working through
a variety of channels which are not integrated. There is a range of
direct transfers from the Ministry of Finance (capital development,
recurrent expenditure, and various discretionary/incentivised
transfers), as well as transfers from line ministries directly to
district departments (for example in health and education). The
latter may involve high levels of donor financing through basket
funds. There is also a range of INGO transfers which may or
may not go through the district government offices. District accounts do show, however, that there has been an overall increase
in revenue – largely from central subventions – from 2000–02 and
there is every reason to expect that this increase has persisted to
the present day, as 2002 was the year in which Lushoto formally
became integrated into the LGRP. (District fiscal dependence on
central transfers has been nationwide since the abolition of the
Development Levy, which was a flat local tax raised and spent by
the district. The *Local Government Restructuring Manual* projects
that reforming councils will require temporary infusions of extra

finance of up to TSH 40 million (PORALG 2000: 0–5). What one can say is that the opportunities for external resource inputs have expanded and, because of the legislation that has enabled the LGRP, districts are now more responsible for the management and allocation of these resources in a way that is unprecedented. This has continued with the creation of a donor basket fund and a Local Government Support Credit, approved by the World Bank in 2005 (World Bank 2004b). This kind of 'responsibilisation' seems analogous to the deepening conduct of custodianship established within the national–global interfaces discussed in the previous chapter.

The increasing focus on resource allocation to the district has been accompanied by concern with district-level 'capacity-building'. One result of this has been an infusion of new graduate public administrators entering Lushoto's local civil service. The purpose of this location is to improve the technical and managerial skills of local government; it will also contribute to the creation of new forms of conduct at the local level. Again, an analogy from the realm of neoliberal governance seems apposite: the infusion of central ministries with technical assistance by the World Bank and bilateral donors. Additionally, Lushoto district government has received a small number of computers equipped with new planning and management software, and district administrators at the higher levels are now tapped in to a constant if infrequent series of national and regional training sessions and workshops. There has been a profusion of workshops, seminars and training sessions, rolled out to key administrative personnel, and then to administrators and councillors generally.

Capacity building of the kind just described has been motivated by concern that financial decentralisation, accompanied by a widening range of possibilities of access to external resources, will cause districts to work as 'sinks' in which public resources drain away from the centre as local officials devise ways of skimming money for their own private purposes. In this light, it makes sense that capacity building has been accompanied by the introduction of new planning processes at the district level. The effect of capacity building has been to introduce new processes of resource management within the District Administration, namely procurement, evaluation, audit, records and outcome orientation. During fieldwork, I was presented with an array of recently created documentation setting out district plans or district-level accounts. Lushoto has a District Development Plan, a Gender Strategic Plan, a series of quarterly account reports which are presented to the District Council, and other planning and account documents. Tendering notices are posted in the district government buildings, the district government reports to the District Council detailing its allocation of expenditure.

Reading this documentation, one is struck by how sharply focused it is on integrating local government with the central language and procedures of the Ministry of Finance and the PRSP. This is partly a result of the fact that good district-level documentation serves the pivotal purpose of expanding and controlling resource transfers from the government of Tanzania. But it is also the result of the narrow epistemology of the planning process in Tanzania, which is the product of the confluence of neoliberalism and new public management. Similar attempts to generate neoliberal practice are written into the LGR: the conduct of responsibility, the habits of audit and workshop, and the repertoire set by new planning instruments and financial reporting. In this view, LGR is substantially the decentralisation of neoliberal practice.

But this view is incomplete. Simply to adopt a notion of 'neoliberalisation by analogy' – LGR as a different level of the same process – would be to impute neoliberalism with its own logic, obscuring agency and practice. It also suggests that there is, at some fundamental level, something 'natural' about neoliberal sociability that is part of the essential code of personhood, which means that neoliberalism doesn't require concerted constructive effort. In fact, this is precisely what it *does* require: consider the extent of the

efforts to infuse central states with neoliberal practice. Thousands
of millions of dollars in credit/aid, thousands of conditionalities,
hundreds of millions of dollars in technical assistance (the World
bank spent $720 million on technical assistance between 1998 and
2008; see *Bretton Woods Update* 60: 5) and training (scholarships,
courses at the World Bank Institute, etc.) over a quarter of a
century simply to produce realms of neoliberal practice at the
centre. This tells us that – in the absence of equally heroic forces
of effort – we should expect that the reform efforts at local level
will have enjoyed limited diffusion and will likely coexist, more or
less comfortably, with other governmental and social practices.

Bricolage practices

Decentralised neoliberal practice in Lushoto is not dominant and
has not liberated neoliberal selves from their 'local' socio-cultural
baggage. Rather, neoliberal practices have been employed by district officials (and others) as and when they find it right, necessary
or appropriate – but not in any plain rational or instrumental sense.
Rather, local officials perceive and evaluate the introduction of
neoliberal practice from grounded places. That is, the existing
practices of authority frame how one might relate to the introduction of neoliberal reforms. It is from these existing social practices
that neoliberalism becomes a resource – a set of possibilities – to
borrow, challenge or ignore. And the resulting bricolage practices
are based on broader articulations of local government with district
society. This section looks at two key themes that emerge from
existing practice.

Development and patrimonialism

One of the cornerstone phrases of Tanzania's post-colonial politics is *maendeleo* (development), which, along with *ujamaa* and
kujitegemea, constituted Tanzania's brand of nationalist developmentalism. The meaning of *maendeleo* has been differently

interpreted (Nyerere 1974; Mercer 2002), but one key political practice that it has encapsulated is the political advocacy of local representatives who aim to capture resources from higher levels of government for their constituency. The ability to 'bring development' to one's home area provided a way of shoring up legitimacy both during the single-party period and into the present day.

In present-day Lushoto, local representation works as follows. There are thirty-two constituencies, each of which has a councillor who represents his or her ward in the District Council, which is located in Lushoto district town. Councillors are elected every four years through universal franchise, which runs along with the national elections. Since 1994, candidates can be supported by any party. Additionally, as a result of national legislation, there are eight 'special seats' in the District Council reserved for women. In Lushoto, all elected councillor seats were retained by men.

Throughout Tanzania's post-colonial history, councillors have needed to maintain legitimacy by being 'development advocates' on behalf of their constituency, even if the control and location of any development resource *within* the ward might be a moot point. Since political and economic liberalisation, competition to be elected as councillor has intensified (Kelsall 2000; Kiondo 1995). Furthermore, one of the first successful measures taken as part of Tanzania's LGR was to reduce the power of the regional commissioner to allocate resources, and to devolve resource allocation down to the district level and to the District Council in particular. As a result, the District Council has become a key focus for those in pursuit of developmental legitimacy.

So, although not an entirely new political practice, developmental politics in Lushoto has been both modified and reinvigorated by decentralisation. In the words of one councillor, there has been a 'development wave since 2000; all councillors want a larger portion of the development budget going to their ward' (Interview, 11 August 2005). 'Bringing the government closer to the people' and pursuing neoliberal reform through infusions of new money have energised practices of development advocacy, the latter having become very robust and institutionalised habits of local political practice. Let us see how this has happened.

As already noted, decentralisation in Tanzania has been based on the districts, and it is the District Councils that are expected to play a pivotal role in terms of both resource management and participation. This is not only to say that councillors represent the *wananchi* (people – an evocative normative term in Tanzania) in their ward, but also that the District Councils should work as a more active influence on the district administration. One can see this formalised in the changes made to the routines of full District Council meetings. The minutes from full Council meetings in Lushoto demonstrate how the District Councils have developed detailed agendas, have attempted to compel various departments of the District Administration to make reports to Council, have created sets of focused minutes, and have integrated reports in the full Council from various standing committees (which are legislated for nationally). The reinvigorated Council meetings contrast with a general view of meetings before neoliberal decentralisation, in which an entire day – and perhaps even part of the night – would be spent discussing issues endlessly and without structure or agreement. Formally, now, the District Administration and the executive (embodied in the District Executive Director) should report to the full Council, which acts as the paramount decision-making body.

The revival of the District Council has produced a routinised opportunity for councillors to lobby and advocate for their own wards. All of the councillors interviewed spent some time explaining that one of their key tasks as local politicians was to argue their case in full Council meetings for support to schools, health care, road improvement, irrigation, and the improvement/construction of wells.

A second centrally legislated process has reinforced Lushoto's developmentalism, which relates closely to the new planning procedures mentioned in the previous section. The District Development Plan, which constitutes the key document to request resources from the government of Tanzania, has a process conditionality built into it, which is that it must be the product of 'participation' throughout the district. This is carried out through a hierarchy of meetings, from the Village Executive Committees, to the Ward Executive Committees and then aggregated, through a process of prioritisation, by the planning department of the District Administration. The District Executive Director (DED) then presents the District Development Plan to a full Council meeting. In effect, what is happening here is that councillors and local representatives of the state (Village Executive Officers, VEOs; and Ward Executive Officers, WEOs) draw up lists of developmental demands (commonly health and education) which they hope will make it through the opaque reworking carried out at the district level by the planning department. If these demands are not carried through into the District Development Plan, councillors have the opportunity to pressure the District Administration during the reporting back to full Council. Failure to do this effectively has a direct impact on the political cachet of the councillor: the VEOs and WEOs 'just shoplist their problems, and expect us to deliver' (local government officer, quoted in Braathen 2003:6).

The importance of this ward–district connection for councillors' attempts to represent themselves as successful development advocates was revealed in interviews with special-seats councillors, because their claims to represent a constituency are relatively weak. One of the main themes that emerged when women were speaking of their marginality as special-seats councillors instead of fully elected councillors derived from the disconnected nature of their mandate. special-seats councillors did not represent a ward; rather, they were selected from a list according to the percentage a party had won in the district elections. Because the Chama Cha Mapinduzi, Party of the Revolution (CCM) has always won all council seats in Lushoto, the local CCM Secretariat selects the women to take up special seats after an intra-party election. The councillors then represent 'women' in general, which, as an abstraction and as a category still subjected to the marginalisation produced by patriarchy, does not allow them to work nearly as well as development advocates. One group of women councillors complained that whenever a special-seats councillor argued for developmental support for women in a certain location, other (male) councillors would rhetorically ask: 'And who do you represent? What district do you represent?' This suggests that special seats have less claim to developmental resources as it is unclear what geographical representation or political unit they speak for; it also suggests that there is an understanding that 'women's needs' are best represented by each district's own councillor. The disempowerment of women councillors is also reinforced by the regulation that only 'ward' councillors can chair standing committees. The de facto result of this is that women councillors have only chaired these committees as caretakers when the existing chair is ill or out of the district. As one woman councillor put it: 'you need a ward to have a voice' (interview, Eva Chamdoma, councillor, August 2005).

Taken together with the developmental logic of the practices of councillors as representatives of their wards, one can identify an intense developmental politics. In fact, much of the practice of local government is infused with the efforts of development advocacy by councillors and village and ward representatives. The revival of the Council has led to an invigorated competition to capture resources from new plans and projects. The technocrats in the district planning and finance departments are regularly pressured to relinquish resources for a range of ward-level projects, and councillors are not impressed by explanations relating to 'resource envelopes' or the hard constraints that define the District Development Plan. In fact, a number of PORALG and consultancy documents refer to the need to 'educate' councillors making resource demands, also expressing concern at the persuasiveness of development politics at the district level and the ability of the full Council to undermine medium-term financially regulated expenditure protocols (Steffensen, Tidemand *et al.* 2004:35). In Lushoto, a recently arrived university economics graduate working as a planning officer characterised the Council as follows:

> Each councillor wants to increase expenditure for their own ward. The planning office needs to educate councillors on government guidelines. For example, the government allocated TSH 15 million for Manoro [ward] and TSH 3 million for Shume [ward]. The district [planning office] gave detailed expenditure plans back [to the Council] but some councillors were angry that Shume got less. Proposals from the district [administration] are usually returned [by the Council] ... This is 'politics' ... councillors refuse to take the money [i.e. approve expenditure plans] if it is very low. (Interview, Andakise Mwakabana, Planning Officer, 16 August 2005)

'Educate' here seems to mean nothing less than the inculcation of new forms of conduct – ones that respect the hegemony of financialised models of resource use, and that see 'politics' as an unhelpful facet of local government reform.

Nevertheless, there is some complementarily here between practices of development advocacy and decentralised neoliberalism. After all, development advocacy is based on the conduct of accountability – bring resources to 'your people'; it is just that neoliberalism sets a new repertoire for this conduct which is both enabling and constraining. The infusion of new resources and initiatives enables efforts to capture development resources for one's ward; but the reforms to produce more transparent, technical and controlled development management make efforts to win discretionary favour more difficult. But there exist realms of political practice outside the District Council in which discretional political practice is very important indeed.

Neo(liberal) patrimonialism

The developmental politics of Lushoto spills over into another area of district politics. This can be introduced through an observation. During six weeks of fieldwork in Lushoto, we tried repeatedly to arrange an interview with the DED. This involved a period almost daily sitting in the waiting room outside his office. It was readily apparent that, more than any other office in the District Administration complex, the DED's office was the busiest. The DED received a constant flow of councillors, who, according to the receptionist, were largely seeking an audience in order to request some form of district support for their ward. Officially, the DED has no discretion to act in this fashion, but the traffic of councillors suggests that, de facto, he did, and that this was a key way in which the DED assured himself of a substantial political presence in the district. His positions as chief executive, chair of the Council Management Team, District Accounting Officer (which means that all central funds are officially submitted through him), and chair of the District Tender Board located him right at the centre of the governance/capacity-building reforms. Because district government is highly dependent on central subventions (Steffensen et al. 2004: xi), the DED's position is structurally highly significant, even if, formally, he is charged with ensuring the implementation of Council decisions.

What is striking here is the contrast with the more open developmental politics of the District Council meetings. The DED's office was a literal and metaphorical illustration of a more opaque and personalised local politics – a 'behind closed doors' set of negotiations and discretionary decisions. Although this form of district politics is the most difficult to research, it constitutes an important sphere of political practice.

There are no statistics and very little written information about corruption in Lushoto. Some council minutes note a few specific cases of the embezzlement of public funds in order to report the disciplinary procedures that were taken. Small-scale bribes by those visiting district offices are commonplace (interview, district administrative officer, 5 August 2005). The Prevention of Corruption Bureau had a district office and occasionally requested information from administrative offices. The District Administration had a 'corruption officer' whose office had no paperwork or computer, and was often open and unoccupied, which suggested that not a great deal of significant activity was happening therein. Tenders and a code of ethics were advertised on the district notice-board and councillors have (as a result of national legislation) been banned from participating in any tenders. Overall, it appeared that anti-corruption measures were being followed procedurally and that small-scale bribes were part of people's negotiations of local state institutions.

A distinction needs to be made here between small- and large-scale corruption. Three members of the Tanzania Women's Association told us that high-level corruption is part of Lushoto's mainstream politics. Tenders remain opaque in how they are awarded and costed, and some considered that the DED gave evasive answers to queries from the Council regarding tenders (interview, Lucas Shemndolwa, vice chair of Council, 4 August 2005). It was an open secret that the election season in Lushoto produced a vigorous circuit of electoral largesse in which electoral patronage would be generated and favours from the local government assured. This activity took place both within the CCM selection process and during the elections proper. Rumours abounded that it was during this period that the DED had assured himself of a new 4×4. Interestingly, the minister for regional administration and local government publicly named the DED of Lushoto as responsible for the rampant misuse of funds, overexpenditure, opaque expenditure reports and illegal payments (*The Citizen*, 3 March 2006).

Lushoto's hardwoods are being illegally felled and evacuated from the district. I was shown two places where forest had been cleared and the tyre tracks of large lorries that led away from these sites. The sites were located in conservation areas. Simply in terms of its scale, this kind of illegal operation is too prominent to be invisible to the District Administration: logging is noisy, takes time, and requires very large vehicles. A number of people in Lushoto, speaking in general conversation and without the information being elicited, referred to a specific local businessman as the entrepreneur carrying out the logging. Occasionally, people would hear the engines of large trucks passing through the district during the early hours of the morning. This was a secretive and illegal form of primitive accumulation that could only be done with the complicity of individuals who could ensure the indifference of the police or other law-enforcing officials.

Those who spoke about the logging all suggested political complicity. And it is difficult to imagine how there could not be high-level support for the activity. It is simply not possible to bring large trucks into Lushoto district (which has one tarmacked road and is highly pedestrianised) without being noticed, far less to drive these through forest tracks, chainsaw trees down, load up the trucks, and drive out of the district. I heard accounts from reliable sources – including a development worker who was born and lived in Lushoto for most of his life – of villagers trying to arrest those felling the trees, only to be faced with police harassment themselves and the quick release of the culprits. We did not pursue the question of how this entrepreneur had established influence within the local state structures because of the sensitivity of the topic (which included allegations of death threats).

Corrupt practice appeared virile and embedded at the heart of district politics. Its connections with other aspects of local political practice were necessarily opaque. Corrupt conduct is based on secrecy and complicity, making it entirely different from neoliberal conduct based on transparency and contract. But these two forms of practice maintain a difficult relationship, rather than a simple opposition. We have seen in Chapter 5 how a key aspect of neoliberal conduct at the central level derived from practices aimed at promoting transparency and combating corruption. But the focus of this chapter has been oriented more towards the 'frontiers' of neoliberalism – the extent and character of neoliberal decentralisation. And this leads us to consider local government and its embeddedness in social practices.

The broader social practices that pertain to any particular country are, of course, manifold. But one is identifiable that is both germane and present (in varying degrees) in all indebted states. This is the practice of accumulation and enrichment by the political-economic elite. Recall that in Chapter 1 it was argued that neoliberalism was not simply capitalism, or capitalism's ideology or 'shell'. Capitalist accumulation is a social relation which has historically emerged and spread in a variety of different contexts. Capitalism is neither intrinsically Western nor neoliberal. Recognising this fact opens the possibility that capitalist accumulation can generate social practices that are not neoliberal and might in fact be, in a sense, *anti*-neoliberal.

This difficult relation between neoliberal practices and the 'corrupt' practices of accumulation generates a problem for advocates of neoliberalism: neoliberal norms are clearly and explicitly based in a capitalist world-view, but a *particular* world-view of socially harmonious progress. The processes of capitalist accumulation based in corrupt practice, zero-sum politics, and various forms of illegal or semi-legal practice (plundering, theft, trafficking) are both violations of neoliberal norms and evidence of a concrete process of capitalist 'development'.

This is the last sense in which this chapter offers the metaphor of a frontier: the problematic interaction of neoliberal practice not only with existing 'local' political practices, but also with high-level and proximate practices of capitalist accumulation. And there is plenty of evidence of this difficult relationship in the emergence of scandals of liberalisation.

Scandals of liberalisation

This section looks at the patchy evidence of the use of corrupt practice within the liberalisation scheme. In Mozambique, Pitcher (2003: 3) argues, there 'has been the model patient envisioned in neoliberal prescriptions'; the World Bank itself judges that the 'Bank's strategy resulted in ... what may be the most successful privatisation programme in Africa' (in Cramer 2001: 80) . However, privatisation has not been carried out in ways that easily fit with the technocratic and apolitical notions of efficiency and the removal of the state from the economy. State-owned companies have been strategically sold, leaving key firms under control of the government, which perceives them as important bases for political support (Pitcher 2003). Those that have been privatised have been subjected to at least underhand and likely corrupt manoeuvres behind the scenes: for example, so-called 'silent privatisations' whereby a tender is not announced and a group of insiders in cahoots with a private company transfer ownership under very concessional conditions (Harrison 1999b). In fact, politically connected private buyers of state property often do not pay the full amount and violate the conditions of sale (Cramer 2001). Perhaps the most prominent case of corrupt privatisation has been the selling off of national banks. Subject to strong conditionalities set down by the World Bank and the IMF, banks have been sold in opaque circumstances, have not accounted for bad debt, and have not established transparent criteria for capital management. Crucially, the leakage of finance from large banks has been a major source of accumulation for a group of businesspeople and politicians, whether these banks are owned publicly or privately. The result of this is an opaque, chaotic and violent privatisation process which has led to the assassination or attempted assassination of journalists, lawyers and bank managers who were not bought into networks of complicity (Hanlon 2002; Fauvet and Mosse 2003).

In Uganda, neoliberal reform has perhaps gone further than anywhere else on the continent. The political will that the Museveni government has displayed in pushing through neoliberal reform is equalled by the unity, stability and centralisation of the state around the presidency. Indeed, the adoption of structural adjustment was supposedly the result of the president's personal decision after discussions within a Presidential Economic Council which effectively acted as a court to Museveni in the early years after gaining power (Lamont 1995: 11–26). Since the mid-1990s, the Ugandan government, regularly attracting plaudits from external sources, has been involved in the illicit plundering of minerals from the Democratic Republic of Congo (DRC) (Reno 2002; UNEP 2002). Tangri and Mwenda give detailed examples of the way in which the plunder of the DRC's resources and corrupt military procurement have thrown suspicion on those centrally placed within the current government (Tangri and Mwenda 2003). A raft of other privatisation scandals (Tangri and Mwenda 2001) also point to the same group of people, clustered around the presidency, and most clearly implicating Museveni's brother.

Tanzania, another success story, also has a series of cases of neoliberal reform, executed on paper but underpinned by corruption, most notably the privatisation and contracting of electricity generation (Cooksey 2002). And, in respect to Tanzania, perhaps the best commentary comes from a World Bank Operations Evaluation Report by the Bank:

> The [World Bank's] Country Assistance Strategy seems to have avoided as much as possible raising the issue of corruption, which is perhaps seen to be politically contentious.... Although corruption in Tanzania is a serious problem, there seems to be an assessment that a more public airing of the problem would hurt rather than help the reform process. (OED World Bank 2001)

At the operational level, some Bank staff recognise that incremental and effective neoliberal reform relies in part on the clientelist strategies of those who champion neoliberalism in a specific national context. This Report was not published. A background paper commissioned by the World Bank for its Uganda Country Assistance Strategy details pervasive corruption, noting that the rising levels of high-level corruption had been known to the Bank since the late 1980s. It also implies that the World Bank and others have not made corruption an issue because the government has maintained macroeconomic reforms and a relatively high rate of economic growth. This Report has remained confidential. In

Mozambique the World Bank has been equivocal in the face of evidence of multi-million-dollar theft, corruption and fraud (Harrison 1999b; Hanlon 2004).

The claim here is not that the World Bank and other external agencies are unconcerned about corruption. Rather, it is simply that advocates of neoliberal reform are far from able to erase other social practices that straddle the highest levels of the state and society. These practices – variously and loosely called corruption, patrimonialism or clientelism – maintain complex, opaque and not entirely coherent interrelations with neoliberal practice. And, as noted earlier, these 'corrupt practices' are just as 'capitalist' as neoliberal practices. Indeed, for some rational-choice economists corruption generates its own market signals.

Conclusion

This chapter has illustrated the fragile frontiers of neoliberal practice outside of the realm of neoliberal governance. Shored up by a constant infusion of dollars, and concentrated in a cloistered community within the ministerial, presidential and developmental buildings of city centres, neoliberal practice has consolidated certain conducts, habits and repertoires. But its remit is uncertain. At the 'local' level, we see how bricolage practices have allowed neoliberal conduct a 'bit part', a place in local governance but by no means a leading role. Furthermore, we have seen that in fact those very same elites that occupy the workshops and donor meetings are also – through allies, families and links with transnational companies – pursuing thoroughly anti-neoliberal social practices.

7

Conclusion:
neoliberalism's prospects

THIS BOOK has argued that neoliberalism is a global project, but not one derived from an inexorable global idea or a logic of capitalism. Rather, it is a project that has emerged within changing social practices, mainly within the states of besieged countries which have been the subjects of intervention by international organisations. This tells us nothing specific about the extent or nature of neoliberal practice; it simply draws our attention to the modalities of social engineering in specific locations. We have done this in regard to Africa with particular attention to those states that have manifested the most neoliberal reform. What we have found is that neoliberal practice emerged out of the combative interventions of structural adjustment. After over twenty years of repeated neoliberal reform efforts, something like a stable realm of neoliberal practice has been established in many African states. But this realm of practice is neither extensive nor entirely stable and settled. Rather, it is only now that advocates of neoliberalism can meaningfully talk of a more widespread state transformation, manifested through decentralisation; and it remains to be seen the extent to which any broader neoliberal sociability might be identified throughout African societies.

Previous chapters have analysed neoliberal practice at the 'meso' level: identifying social practices in the conducts, habits and repertoires of state officials, international donor/creditors, and a bundle of related intellectuals, as well as some civil society organisations. We have seen how a global context of neoliberal rule-making and institutional interconnection provides a framing for various national practices. Within states, we have seen how reform programmes (SAP, PRSP etc.), governance techniques (new public management, output oriented budgeting etc.), forms of sociability (workshops, meetings with donors etc.), resource constraints and incentives (public expenditure tracking, World Bank/IMF funding attached to PRSPs etc.), discursive norms (transparency, accountability, efficiency etc.) collectively constitute neoliberal social engineering. This required – and continues to require – considerable and concerted effort.

What, then, of neoliberalism's prospects? One key insight that emerges from this book is that external intervention largely characterised by coercive intent does not induce changes in practice; rather, it simply produces bare conformity in equal measure to the extent to which threats and conditionalities are imposed. Thus, neoliberal practice is extant largely in the ways in which it has become part of African governance. It will be in the resilience of neoliberal governance – something which will vary from country to country – that neoliberalism's strength will lie. But it is, of course, clear that neoliberal social engineering remains substantially unrealised: local government reform and other aspects of development policy (for example, micro-credit schemes) are only just beginning to attempt a more ambitious project of social transformation. And prospects and results to date hardly suggest immediate and/or universal 'progress'. Social practices are 'thick' phenomena, and their transformation perhaps requires a great deal of violence, and certainly requires protracted social engineering by effective state institutions.

Beyond an assessment of neoliberal social engineering in terms of its own progress to date, there are also other factors that should be accounted for. First, as suggested throughout the book, changing social relations of capitalism maintain a complex relation with neoliberal reform. Neoliberalism might be interpreted as an enabling practice for capitalist development, but capitalist development neither requires neoliberalism nor necessarily promotes it. Capitalist accumulation has effectively attached itself to a variety of other forms of social practice. As in many other parts of the world and different times, accumulation has relied upon kinship and the hierarchies and obligations often contained therein; accumulation has also emerged out of practices of dispossession and violence. In a country like Uganda, neoliberal reform is relatively advanced, and capitalist accumulation has been virile. But the latter has been realised through widespread practices of fraud, corruption and trickery, leading to a popular understanding of capitalism as 'fake development'.

And, of course, global capitalism is ever-changing. The dominance of the neoliberal capitalist model championed by the USA, the World Bank, the IMF and others has been undermined both by the emergence of China and other significant and unorthodox economies, and by the financial instability and recession caused by poorly regulated aggressive lending by mainly American private financial institutions. Neoliberalism no longer connotes 'good conduct' in the way that it used to. It is unclear how and to what extent the global recession will affect African countries in the medium term, but it is certainly the case that the global hegemony of neoliberalism is weakened.

Alternative development models may or may not emerge in the spaces allowed by a weakened global disposition. These models might derive from existing social practices within African societies, which might serve as a more robust base for progressive state action, more engaged state–society interactions, and stronger senses of sovereignty and national self-interest.

Global recession

Since 2007, the global economy has gone into recession: there has been a sustained slowdown in rates of growth, falling international trade and commodity prices, and the availability of finance has radically decreased. Clearly this is having manifold effects on African states. The 'boom' commodities of the 1990s and early 2000s – oil, copper, cut flowers, and exotic fruits and vegetables – are now falling in price. It is likely that remittances will be falling and that other economic sectors – for example, luxury tourism – will be shrinking.

But how might global recession be affecting neoliberalism's global project to induce market-conforming social practices? Most obviously, recession undermines the legitimacy of this project. There is evidence that African civil society organisations and some within governments are questioning neoliberalism's status as 'meta development' (Chapter 4) in which all development issues, projects and actions are framed as questions of marketisation. Global recession undermines the African exceptionalism discussed in Chapter 1 in which globalisation's most socially damaging effects are 'provincialised' as being specifically a product of Africa, not of globalisation itself. The quotation that introduces Chapter 1 is especially germane here: Lagos serves as a metaphor to illustrate how capitalism can produce informality, social hardship and disorder not simply in Africa but *anywhere*. Homelessness, destitution, massive urban deprivation, and the failure of social infrastructure can be found in the West with increasing prominence as unemployment and repossessions rise. The issue is simple: if those states strongly advocating neoliberal social engineering are currently enduring significant social and economic problems themselves, on what basis does the model claim legitimacy?

There is a further aspect of the recession which is likely to undermine neoliberal social engineering. Aid budgets – both bilateral and through the World Bank and the IMF – are likely to fall. This will have serious effects – not necessarily on African's well-being, but rather on the ability of specific social practices to be introduced. Throughout this book, we have seen how neoliberal social practices have been underpinned by a 'resource effort'; that is, changes in government structures, new management techniques, training, and so on, have required millions of dollars in external finance. If the funds to promote these changes are less available, the prospects for neoliberal reform rest increasingly heavily on the assumption that all individuals are, in essence, liberal selves. As we have seen, this is an essentialism which ignores the cultural and social embeddedness of Africans as selves and collectivities. This is precisely why this book argues that neoliberal 'progress' has been characterised by strong-arm conditionality, massive resource input and halting progress. With less aid and with less evidence that the free market 'works', it is difficult to see how neoliberal social engineering can continue with its onward march.

An uncertain conjuncture

This is not the point at which one can straightforwardly set out alternatives to neoliberalism; nor is it possible – even though it is desirable – to announce an end to neoliberalism. But it is important to recognise that there has not been such a degree of *uncertainty* for the neoliberal project in Africa since the early 1980s. This is a time – perhaps just a moment – in which policy unorthodoxy might increase.

It is most likely that this unorthodoxy will bring to the foreground the fact that African political economies are extremely diverse. Neoliberalism was, in a sense, nothing more than a template, imposed upon all African states with very little variation. It rendered Africa a single space with a set of generic 'problems' and 'solutions'. If we are seeing a waning of the political purchase of neoliberalism, it is likely that states will more clearly develop different kinds of development politics. Intellectually and politically, there are many ways of approaching development outside of the neoliberal framework (Chang and Grabel 2004). These 'alternative developments' might feed into specific African contexts, or relatively novel forms of development strategy might emerge.

But we cannot be too sanguine about a thousand flowers blooming in the wake of a declining neoliberal age. African states are not straightforwardly the expressions of popular nationalisms; indeed many states have oppressed and exploited their peoples. If the World Bank, the IMF, and associated donors and policy advocates retreat, governments might pursue more aggressively strategies of dispossession, patriarchal neotraditionalism and simple self-aggrandisement. Aid-dependent states might find it increasingly difficult to maintain even a basic social order.

It is also possible that we might witness yet another neoliberal mutation. As we have seen, neoliberal social practice has been 'layered': it has involved both coercive interventions and more 'involved' manipulations of governance practice, drawing on institutionalism, liberal democratic politics, poverty reduction, and so on. Neoliberalism's elasticity derives precisely from the fact that it is manifest in repeated attempts to change the habits, conducts and repertoires of its subjects. It might be possible for the World Bank, the IMF and others to find ways of adapting neoliberal practices to a more austere age, perhaps relying on new financial mechanisms, or less aid-driven models of social change. In the event that this happens, it is important not to analyse these innovations critically as idea-driven, or as perfectly designed schemes to maintain the hegemony of the free market; neoliberalism's persistence and its flexibility should be evaluated centrally by the nature of the social practices it produces.

References

Abrahamsen, R. (2000) *Disciplining Democracy: Development Discourse and Good Government in Africa*, Zed Books, London.

Abrahamsen, R. (2004) 'The Power of Partnerships in Global Governance', *Third World Quarterly*, vol. 25, no. 8: 1453–67.

Adam, C., and J. Gunning (2002) 'Redesigning the Aid Contract: Donors' Use of Performance Indicators in Uganda', *World Development*, vol. 30, no. 12: 2045–56.

Adepoju, A. (ed.) (1993) *The Impact of Structural Adjustment on the Population of Africa: The Implications for Education, Health and Employment*, James Currey, London.

African Development Bank (2006) *African Development Report*, Oxford University Press, Oxford.

Agamben, G. (2005) *Homo Sacer: Sovereign Power and Bare Life*, Stanford University Press, Stanford CA.

Akuoko-Frimpong, H. (1994) 'Ghana: Capacity Building for Change', in L. Picard and M. Garrity (eds), *Policy Reform for Sustainable Development in Africa: The Institutional Imperative*, Lynne Rienner, London and Boulder CO: 19–35.

Amenga-Etego, R., and S. Grusky (2005) 'The New Face of Conditionalities: The World Bank and Water Privatisation in Ghana', in D.A. McDonald and G. Ruiters (eds), *The Age of the Commodity: Water Privatisation in Southern Africa*, Earthscan, London: 275–89.

Appaih, K.A. (1993) *In My Father's House: Africa in the Philosophy of Culture*, Oxford University Press, Oxford.

Asante, M.K. (2007) *An Afrocentric Manifesto: Toward an African Renaissance*, Polity Press, Oxford.

Ayers, A. (2006) 'Demystifying Democratisation: The Global Constitution of (Neo)liberal polities in Africa', *Third World Quarterly*, vol. 27, no. 2: 321–38.

Baker, B. (1998) 'The Class of 1990: How Have the Autocratic Leaders of Sub-Saharan Africa Fared under Democratization?', *Third World Quarterly* vol. 19, no. 1: 115–27.

Barkan, J., J.D. Simba Kayunga, S. Ng'ethe and N. Titsworth (2004) 'The Political Economy of Uganda: The Art of Managing a Donor-financed Neo-patrimonial State', World Bank Background Paper (confidential), Kampala.

Bauer, P. (1972) *Dissent on Development*, Harvard University Press, Cambridge MA.

Bayart, J.F. (1991) 'Finishing with the Idea of the Third World: The Concept of the Political Trajectory', in J. Manor (ed.), *Rethinking Third World Politics*, Longman, London: 51–71.

Bayart, J.F. (1993) *The State in Africa: The Politics of the Belly*, Heinemann, London.

Bayliss, K., and D. Hall (2002) *Another PSIRU Critique of Another Version of the World Bank Private Sector Development Strategy*, Public Services International Research Unit (PSIRU), London.

Beckman, B. (1993) 'The Liberation of Civil Society: Neo-liberal Ideology and Political Theory', *Review of African Political Economy*, vol. 20, no. 58: 20–33.

Bello, W. (1993) *Dark Victory: US Structural Adjustment and Global Poverty*, Pluto Press, London.

Bernstein, H. (2004) 'Considering Africa's Agrarian Questions', *Historical Materialism*, vol. 12, no. 4: 115–44.

Bhabha, H. (2004) *Location of Culture*, Routledge, London.

Bigsten, A., and S. Kayizzi-Mugerwa (1999) *Crisis, Adjustment and Growth in Uganda: A Study of Adaptation in an African Economy*, Macmillan, Houndmills.

Blyth, M. (2007) 'Powering, Puzzling, or Persuading? The Mechanisms of Building Institutional Orders', *International Studies Quarterly*, vol. 51, no. 4: 761–77.

Bond, P. (2004) *Against Global Apartheid: South Africa Meets the World Bank, IMF and International Finance*, Zed Books, London.

Bond, P. (2005) 'US Empire and South African Subimperialism', in L. Panitch and C. Leys (eds), *Socialist Register 2005: The Empire Reloaded*, Merlin Press, London: 218–39.

Boone, C. (2003) *Political Topographies of the African State: Rural Authority and Institutional Choice*, Cambridge University Press, Cambridge.

Bourdieu, P. (1977) *Outline of a Theory of Practice*, Cambridge University Press, Cambridge.

Bourdieu, P. (1993) *Firing Back: Against the Tyranny of the Market*, New Press, New York.

Bourdieu, P. (1998) 'The Essence of Neoliberalism', *Le Monde Diplomatique*, 12 August, http://mondediplo.com/1998/12/08bourdieu, accessed May 2008.

Braathen, E. (2003) 'Social Funds – Support of Obstacle to Local Government Reform', NIBR Working Paper no. 118, Norwegian Institute for Urban and Regional Research (NIBR), Oslo.

Bracking, S. (2001) 'The Lesotho Highlands Corruption Trial', *Review of African Political Economy*, vol. 28, no. 88: 302–6.

Bracking, S. (2004) 'Neoclassical and Structural Analysis of Poverty: Winning the "Economic Kingdom" for the Poor in Southern Africa', *Third World Quarterly*, vol. 25, no. 5: 887–901.

Bracking, S. (2009) *Money and Power: The Great Predators in the Political Economy of Development*, London, Pluto.

Bracking, S., and G. Harrison (2003) 'Africa, Imperialism and New Forms of Accumulation', *Review of African Political Economy*, vol. 30, no. 95: 5–10.

Brass, T. (1997) 'The Agrarian Myth, the "New" Populism and the "New" Right', *Journal of Peasant Studies*, vol. 24, no. 4: 201–46.

Brautigam, D. (2003) 'Close Encounters: Chinese Business Networks as Industrial Catalysts in Sub-Saharan Africa', *African Affairs* vol. 102, no. 408: 447–67.

Brenner, N., and N. Theodore (2002) 'Cities and the Geographies of "Actually Existing Neoliberalism"', *Antipode*, vol. 34, no. 3: 349–79.

Brenner, R. (1998) 'The Economics of Global Turbulence', *New Left Review*, Series I, no. 229: 1–265.

Brett, E.A. (2008) 'State Failure and Success in Uganda and Zimbabwe: The Logic of Political Decay and Reconstruction in Africa', *Journal of Development Studies*, vol. 44, no. 3: 339–64.

Bretton Woods Organisation (various issues) *Bretton Woods Update*, www.brettonwoodsproject.org.

Brohman, J. (1995a) 'Universalism, Eurocentrism, and Ideological Bias in Development Studies', *Third World Quarterly*, vol. 16, no. 1: 121–40.

Brohman, J. (1995b) 'Economism and Critical Silences in Development Studies: A Theoretical Critique of Neoliberalism', *Third World Quarterly*, vol. 16, no. 2: 297–318.

Brohman, J. (2005c) *Popular Development: Thinking the Theory and Practice of Development*, Blackwell, Oxford.

Brown, E., and J. Cloke (2004) 'Neoliberal Reform, Governance and Corruption in the South: assessing the International Anti-corruption Crusade', *Antipode*, vol. 36, no. 2: 273–94.

Brown, S. (2005) 'Foreign Aid and Democracy Promotion: Lessons from Africa', *European Journal of Development Research*, vol. 17, no. 2: 179–98.

Brown, W. (2006) 'Africa and International Relations: A Comment on IR Theory, Anarchy and Statehood', *Review of International Studies*, vol. 32, no. 1: 119–43.

Bryceson, D., C. Kay and J. Mooij (eds) (2000) *Disappearing Peasantries? Rural Labour in Africa, Asia, and Latin America*, Intermediate Technology Publications, London.

Bush, R. (2004) 'Undermining Africa', *Historical Materialism*, vol. 12, no. 4: 173–203.

Cahn, J. (1993) 'Challenging the New Imperial Authority: The World Bank and the Democratization of Development', *Harvard Human Rights Journal*, vol. 6, no. 1: 159–94.

Callaghy, T. (1996) 'Africa Falling Off the Map', *Current History*, vol. 93, no. 579: 31–6.

Callaghy, T. (2002) 'Innovation in the Sovereign Debt Regime: From the Paris Club to Enhanced HIPC and Beyond', Operations Evaluation Department Working Paper, World Bank, Washington DC.

Callaghy, T., R. Kassimir and R. Latham (eds) (2001) *Intervention and Transnationalism in Africa: Global–Local Networks of Power*, Cambridge University Press, Cambridge.

Cammack, P. (2002) 'Neoliberalism, the World Bank and the New Politics of Development', in U. Kothari and M. Minogue (eds), *Development Theory and Practice: Critical Perspectives*, Palgrave, Basingstoke: 157–78.

Campbell, B.K., and J. Loxley (1989) *Structural Adjustment in Africa*, Macmillan, Basingstoke.

Campbell, H., and H. Stein (eds) (1992) *Tanzania and the IMF: The Dynamics of Liberalization*, Westview Press, Boulder CO.

Campbell, J. (1995) *Understanding John Dewey*, Open Court, Chicago.

Campbell, J. (2001) 'Institutional Analysis and the Role of Ideas in Political Economy', in J. Campbell and O. Pedersen (eds), *The Rise of Neoliberalism and Institutional Analysis*, Princeton University Press, Princeton: 159–89.

Campbell, J., and O. Pedersen (eds) (2001) *The Rise of Neoliberalism and Institutional Analysis*, Princeton University Press, Princeton.

Castree, N. (2006) 'Commentary: from Neoliberalism to Neoliberalisation: Consolations, Confusions, and Necessary Illusions', *Environment and Planning A*, vol. 38, no. 1: 1–6.

Chabal, P. (1992) *Political Domination in Africa*, Cambridge: Cambridge University Press.

Chang, H.J. (2002) 'Breaking the Mould: An Institutionalist Political Economy Alternative to the Neoliberal Theory of the Market and the State', *Cambridge Journal of Economics*, vol. 26, no. 5: 539–99.

Chang, H.J. and I. Grabel (2004) *Reclaiming Development: An Alternative Economic Policy Manual*, London: Zed Books.

Chazan, N., P. Lewis, R. Mortimer, D. Rothchild and S.J. Stedman (1999) *Politics and Society in Contemporary Africa*, Lynne Rienner, Boulder CO.

Chomsky, N. (1998) *Profit over People: Neoliberalism and Global Order*, Seven Stories Press, New York.

Chorev, N. (2005) 'The Institutional Project of Neo-liberal Globalisation: The Case of the WTO', *Theory and Society*, vol. 34, no. 5: 317–55.

Clapham, C. (1996) *Africa and the International System*, Cambridge University Press, Cambridge.

Clarke, S. (2005) 'The Neoliberal Theory of Society', in A. Saad-Filho and D. Johnston (eds), *Neoliberalism: A Critical Reader*, Pluto Press, London: 50–59.

Cohen, J., and J. Rogers (1992) 'Secondary Associations and Democratic Governance', *Politics and Society*, vol. 20, no. 4: 393–472.

Colclough, C. (1996) 'Education and the Market: Which Parts of the Neoliberal Solution Are Correct?', *World Development*, vol. 24, no. 6: 589–610.

Comaroff, J. (2006) 'Beyond Bare Life: AIDS, (Bio)politics and the Neoliberal Order', *Public Culture*, vol. 19, no. 1: 197–219.

Comaroff, J., and J.L. Comaroff (2000) 'Millennial Capitalism: First Thoughts on a Second Coming', *Public Culture*, vol. 12, no. 2: 291–343.

Commission for Africa (2005) *Our Common Interest*, www.commissionforafrica.org/english/report/introduction.html, accessed May 2008.

Cooke B. (2003) 'A New Continuity with Colonial Administration: Participation in Development Management', *Third World Quarterly*, vol. 24, no. 1: 47–61.

Cooke, B., and U. Kothari (2001) 'The Case of Participation as Tyranny', in B. Cooke and U. Kothari (eds), *Participation: The New Tyranny?*, Zed Books, London: 1–15.

Cooksey, B. (2002) 'The Power and the Vainglory: Anatomy of a $100 Million Malaysian IPP in Tanzania', in K.S. Jomo (ed.), *Ugly Malaysians? South–South Investments Abused*, Centre for Black Research, Durban.

Cooper, F. (2001) 'What Is the Concept of Globalization Good For? An African Historian's Perspective', *African Affairs*, vol. 100, no. 399: 189–213.

Cornia, G., R. Jolly and F. Stewart (1987) *Adjustment with a Human Face*, Vol. 1: *Protecting the Vulnerable and Promoting Growth*, Clarendon Press, Oxford.

Cowen, M., and R. Shenton (1996) *Doctrines of Development*, Routledge, London.

Craig, D., and D. Porter (2005) 'The Third Way and the Third World: Poverty Reduction and Social Inclusion Strategies in the Rise of "Inclusive" Liberalism', *Review of International Political Economy* vol. 12, no. 2: 226–64.

Craig, D., and G. Cotterell (2007) 'Periodising Neoliberalism?', *Policy and Politics*, vol. 35, no. 3: 497–514.

Cramer, C. (2001) 'Mozambique: A "Hospital Pass?"', *Journal of Southern African Studies*, vol. 27, no. 1: 79–103.

Cramer, C., C. Oya and J. Sender (2008) 'Lifting the Blinkers: A New View of Power, Diversity and Poverty in Mozambican Rural Labour Markets', *Journal of Modern African Studies*, vol. 46, no. 3: 361–92.

Crawford, G. (1997) 'Foreign Aid and Political Conditionality: Issues of Effectiveness and Consistency', *Democratization*, vol. 4, no. 3: 69–108.

Crawford, G. (2005) 'The European Union and Democracy Promotion in Africa: The Case of Ghana', *European Journal of Development Research*, vol. 17, no. 4: 571–600.

Davidson, B. (1992) *The Black Man's Burden: The Curse of the Nation State*, James Currey, London.

De Soto, H. (2001) *The Mystery of Capital*, Black Swan, New York.

Demmers, J., A.E. Férnandez Jilberto and B. Hogenboom (eds) (2004) *Good Governance in the Era of Neoliberalism*, Routledge, London.

Dewey, J. (1922) *Human Nature and Conduct*, Dover, New York.

Dewey, J. (1929) *The Quest for Certainty: A Study of the Relation of Knowledge and Action*, Minton, Balch, New York.

Duffield, M. (2001) *Global Governance and the New Wars: The Merging of Development and Security*, Zed Books, London.

Duménil, G., and D. Lévy (2001) 'Costs and Benefits of Neoliberalism', *Review of International Political Economy*, vol. 8, no. 4: 578–607.

Duménil, G., and D. Lévy (2004) *Capital Resurgent: Roots of the Neoliberal Revolution*, Harvard University Press, Cambridge MA.

Eade, D. (2007) 'Editorial', *Development in Practice*, vol. 17, nos 4–5: 679–81.

Easterly, W. (2007) *The White Man's Burden: Why the West's Efforts to Aid the Rest Have Done So Much Ill and So Little Good*, Oxford University Press, Oxford.

Edwards, M. (1999). 'Enthusiasts, Tacticians and Sceptics: The World Bank, Civil Society and Social Capital', manuscript.

Einhorn, J. (2001) 'The World Bank's Mission Creep', *Foreign Affairs*, vol. 80, no. 5: 22–35.

Elbadawi, I., and Nicholas Sambanis (2000) 'Why Are There So Many Civil Wars in Africa? Understanding and Preventing Violent Conflict', *Journal of African Economies*, vol. 9, no. 3: 224–69.

Ellis, F. (2000) *Rural Livelihoods and Diversity in Developing Countries*, Oxford University Press, Oxford.

Elster, J. (1986) *An Introduction to Karl Marx*, Cambridge University Press, Cambridge.

England, K., and K. Ward (2002) 'Reflections on Neoliberalisation', in K. England and K. Ward (eds), *Neoliberalisation: States, Networks, Peoples*, Blackwell, Oxford: 248–71.

Engel, U., and G. Rye Olsen (eds) (2005) *Africa and the North: Between Globalization and Marginalization*, Routledge, London.

Evans, A., and E. Ngalwea (2003) 'Tanzania', *Development Policy Review*, vol. 21, no. 2: 271–87.

Fauvet, P., and M. Mosse (2003) *Carlos Cardoso: Telling the Truth in Mozambique*, Double Storey, Cape Town.

Feierman, S. (1974) *The Shambaa Kingdom*, Kapsel, Dar es Salaam.

Feierman, S. (1990) *Peasant Intellectuals: Anthropology and History in Tanzania*, University of Wisconsin Press, Madison.

Feierman, S. (2005) 'On Socially Composed Knowledge: Reconstructing a Shambaa Royal Ritual', in G.H. Maddox and J.L. Giblin (eds), *In Search of a Nation: Histories of Authority and Dissidence in Tanzania*, James Currey, Oxford: 14–33.

Ferguson, J. (1994) *The Anti-politics Machine: 'Development', Depoliticisation and Bureaucratic Power in Lesotho*, University of Minnesota Press, London.

Ferguson, J. (1995) 'From African Socialism to Scientific Capitalism: Reflections on the Legitimation Crisis in IMF-Ruled Africa', in D. Moore and G. Schmitz (eds), *Debating Development Discourse*, Palgrave, Houndmills: 129–49.

Ferguson, J. (2006) *Global Shadows: Africa in the Neoliberal World Order*, Duke University Press, Durham NC.

Ferguson, J. (2007) 'Formalities of Poverty: Thinking about Social Assistance in South Africa', *African Studies Review*, vol. 50, no. 2: 71–86.

Festenstein, M. (2002) 'Pragmatism's Boundaries', *Millennium*, vol. 31, no. 3: 549–71.

Fine, B. (1999) 'The Developmental State is Dead – Long Live Social Capital', *Development and Change* vol. 30, no. 1: 1–21.

Fine, B. (2000) *Social Capital versus Social Theory: Political Economy and Social Science at the Turn of the Millennium*, Routledge, London.

Fine, B., C. Lapvitsas and J. Pincus (eds) (2001) *Development Policy in the Twenty-first Century: Beyond the Post-Washington Consensus*, Routledge, London.

Fisher, W., and T. Ponniah (2003) *Another World is Possible: Popular Alternatives to Globalization at the World Social Forum*, Zed Books, London.

Fraser, A. (2005) 'Poverty Reduction Strategy Papers: Now Who Calls the Shots?', *Review of African Political Economy*, vol. 32, nos. 104–5: 317–40.

Freund, B. (1988) *The Making of Contemporary Africa*, Macmillan, Houndmills.

Friedman, T. (2000) *The Lexus and the Olive Tree: Understanding Globalization*, London, HarperCollins.

Frynas, J. (1998) 'Political Instability and Business: Focus on Shell in Nigeria', *Third World Quarterly*, vol. 19, no. 3: 457–78.

Gamble, A., and T. Payne (eds) (1996) *Regionalism and World Order*, Palgrave Macmillan, Houndmills.

George, S., and F. Sabelli (1994) *Faith and Credit: The World Bank's Secular Empire*, Penguin Books, London.

Geschiere, P., and F. Nyamnjoh (2000) 'Capitalism and Autochthony: The Seesaw of Mobility and Belonging', *Public Culture*, vol. 12, no. 2: 423–52.

Ghai, D. (ed.) (1991) *The IMF and the South: The Social Impact of Crisis and Adjustment*, Zed Books, London.

Gibb, R. (2004) 'Developing Countries and Market Access: The Bitter-sweet Taste of the European Union's Sugar Policy in Southern Africa', *Journal of Modern African Studies*, vol. 42, no. 4: 563–88.

Gibbon, P. (ed.) (1993) *Social Change and Economic Reform in Africa*, Scandinavian Institute of African Studies (SIAS), Uppsala.

Gibbon, P. (1996) 'Zimbabwe', in P. Engberg-Pedersen, P. Gibbon, P. Raikes and L. Udsholt (eds), *Limits of Adjustment in Africa*, James Currey, London: 347–93.

Gibbon, P., K. Havnevik, and K. Hermele (1993) *A Blighted Harvest: The World Bank and African Agriculture in the 1980s*, James Currey, London.

Gibbon, P., and S. Ponte (2005) *Trading Down: Africa, Value Chains and the Global Economy*, Temple University Press, Philadelphia.

Gill, S. (1995) 'Globalisation, Market Civilisation, and Disciplinary Neoliberalism', *Millennium*, vol. 24, no. 3: 399–423.

Glinavos, I. (2008) 'Neoliberal Law: Unintended Consequences of Market-friendly Law Reforms', *Third World Quarterly*, vol. 29, no. 6: 1087–99.

Gould, J., and J. Ojanen (2003) 'Merging the Circle: The Politics of Tanzania's Poverty Reduction Strategy', Policy Paper no. 2/2003, Institute of Development Studies, University of Helsinki.

Gould, J. (ed.) (2005) *The New Conditionality: The Politics of Poverty Reduction Strategies*, Zed Books, London.

Gowan, P. (1995) 'Neoliberal Theory and Practice for Eastern Europe', *New Left Review*, series I, no. 213: 3–61.

Green, M. (2003) 'Globalizing Development in Tanzania', *Critique of Anthropology*, vol. 23, no. 2: 123–43.

Guyer, J. (2004) *Marginal Gains: Monetary Transactions in Atlantic Africa*, University of Chicago Press, Chicago.

Hanlon, J., and T. Smart (2008) *Do Bicycles Equal Development in Mozambique?*, James Currey, London.

Hanlon, J. (2000) 'How Much Debt Should Be Cancelled?', *Journal of International Development*, vol. 12, no. 6: 877–901.

Hanlon, J. (2002) 'Bank Corruption Becomes Site of Struggle in Mozambique', *Review of African Political Economy*, vol. 29, no. 91: 53–72.

Hanlon, J (2004) 'Do Donors Promote Corruption? The Case of Mozambique', *Third World Quarterly*, vol. 25, no. 4: 747–63.

Hanlon, J. (2006) '"Illegitimate" Loans: Lenders, Not Borrowers Are Responsible', *Third World Quarterly,* vol. 27, no. 2: 211–26.

Hanson, M., and J. Hentz (1999) 'Neocolonialism and Neoliberalism in South Africa and Zambia', *Political Science Quarterly*, vol. 114, no. 3: 479–502.

Harman, C. (2008) 'Theorising Neoliberalism', *International Socialism* 117: 87–121.

Harrison, G. (1999a) 'Mozambique between Two Elections: A Political Economy of Transition', *Democratization*, vol. 6, no. 4: 166–80.

Harrison, G. (1999b) 'Corruption as "Boundary Politics": The State, Democratization, and Mozambique's Unstable Liberalization', *Third World Quarterly*, vol. 20, no. 3: 523–36.

Harrison, G. (2001) 'Administering Market-Friendly Growth? Liberal Populism and the World Bank's Involvement in Administrative Reform in Sub-Saharan Africa', *Review of International Political Economy*, vol. 8, no. 3: 528–48.

Harrison, G. (2002) *Issues in the Contemporary Politics of Sub-Saharan Africa. The Dynamics of Struggle and Resistance*, Palgrave, Basingstoke.

Harrison, G. (2004) *The World Bank and Africa: The Construction of Governance States*, Routledge, London.

Harrison, G. (2005) 'Economic Faith, Social Project, and a Misreading of African Society: The Travails of Neoliberalism in Africa', *Third World Quarterly*, vol. 26, no. 8: 1303–20.

Harrison, G., and S. Mulley with D. Holtom (2009) 'Tanzania: A Genuine Case of Recipient Leadership in the Aid System?', in L. Whitfield (ed.), *The Politics of Aid*, Oxford University Press, Oxford: 271–99.

Harriss, J. (2002) *Depoliticizing Development: The World Bank and Social Capital*, Anthem Press, London.

Harriss, J., J. Hunter and C. Lewis (eds) (1995) *The New Institutional Economics and Third World Development*, Routledge, London.

Harvey, C. (1991) 'Recovery from Macroeconomic Disaster in Sub-Saharan Africa', in C. Colclough and J. Manor (eds), *States or Markets? Neoliberalism and the Development Policy Debate*, Clarendon Press, Oxford: 121–47.

Harvey, D. (2005) *A Brief History of Neoliberalism*, Oxford University Press, Oxford.

Harvey, D. (2007) 'Neoliberalism as Creative Destruction', *The Annals of the American Academy of Political and Social Science*, vol. 610, no. 1: 21–44.

Havnevik, K.J. (1987) *The IMF and the World Bank in Africa: Conditionality, Impact, and Alternatives*, Scandinavian Institute of African Studies, Uppsala and Stockholm.

Hay, C. (2004) 'The Normalising Role of Rationalist Assumptions in the Institutional Embedding of Neoliberalism', *Economy and Society*, vol. 33, no. 4: 500–27.

Hay, C., and D. Marsh (1999) *Demystifying Globalization*, St. Martin's Press, New York.

Hearn, J. (1999) 'Foreign Political Aid, Democratisation, and Civil Society in Uganda in the 1990s', CBR Working Paper no. 53, Centre for Basic Research (CBR), Kampala.

Hearn, J. (2007) 'African NGOs: The New Compradors?', *Development and Change*, vol. 38, no. 6: 1095–110.

Helleiner, G. (1999) 'Changing Aid Relationships in Tanzania', paper for the Tanzania Consultative Group Meeting, 3 May, Dar es Salaam.

Helleiner, G., T. Killick, N. Lipumba, B. Ndulu and K. Svendsen (1995) *Report of Independent Advisors on Development Cooperation Issues between Tanzania and Its Donors*, Royal Danish Ministry of Foreign Affairs, Copenhagen.

Herbst, J. (2000) *States and Power in Africa: Comparative Lessons in Authority and Control*, Princeton University Press, Princeton.

Hermele, K. (1988) 'Guerra e Estabilização. Uma análise a médio prazo do Programa de Recuperação Económica de Moçambique (PRE)', *Revista Internacional de Estudos Africanos* 8/9: 339–49.

Heron, T. (2008) 'Globalisation, Neoliberalism and the Exercise of Agency', *International Journal of Politics, Culture and Society*, vol. 20, no. 1: 85–101.

Hewitt, V. (2006) 'A Cautionary Tale: Colonial and Postcolonial Conceptions of Good Government and Democratisation in Africa', *Commonwealth and Comparative Politics*, vol. 44, no. 1: 41–61.

Hobson, J.M., and L. Seabrooke (eds) (2007) *Everyday Politics of the World Economy*, Cambridge University Press, Cambridge.

Hodgson, G. (2004) 'Reclaiming Habit for Institutional Economics', *Journal of Economic Psychology*, vol. 25, no. 5: 651–60.

Holtom, D. (2005) 'Reconsidering the Power of the IFIs: Tanzania and the World Bank, 1978–1985', *Review of African Political Economy*, vol. 32, no. 106: 549–69.

Hovden, E., and E. Keene (eds) (2001) *The Globalization of Liberalism*, Palgrave Macmillan, Houndmills.

Howe, J. (1998) *Afrocentrism*, Verso, London.

Hutchful, E. (1994) '"Smoke and Mirrors": The World Bank's Social Dimensions of Adjustment (SDA) Programme', *Review of African Political Economy*, vol. 21, no. 62: 569–84.

Jubilee Research (2003) *The Real Progress Report on HIPC*, New Economics Foundation, London.

Kamat, S. (2004) 'The Privatisation of Public Interest: Theorising NGO Discourse in a Neoliberal Era', *Review of International Political Economy*, vol. 11, no. 1: 155–76.

Kaplinski, R. (2005) *Globalization, Poverty and Inequality: Between a Rock and a Hard Place*, Polity Press, Cambridge.

Kasfir, N. (ed.) (1998) *Civil Society and Democracy in Africa: Critical Perspectives*, Frank Cass, London.

Kelsall, T. (2000) 'Governance, Local Politics, and Districtization in Tanzania: The 1988 Arumeru Tax Revolt', *African Affairs*, vol. 99, no. 397: 533–53.

Kingfisher, C., and J. Maskovsky (2008) 'The Limits of Neoliberalism', *Critique of Anthropology*, vol. 28, no. 2: 115–26.

Kiondo, A. (1995) 'When the State Withdraws: Local Development, Politics and Liberalisation in Tanzania', in P. Gibbon (ed.), *Liberalised Development in Tanzania*, Nordic Africa Institute, Uppsala: 109–77.

Klare, M., and D. Volman (2006) 'The African "Oil Rush" and US National Security', *Third World Quarterly*, vol. 27, no. 2: 609–28.

Klitgaard, R. (1988) *Controlling Corruption*, University of California Press, Berkeley.

Klitgaard, R. (1989) 'Incentive Myopia', *World Development*, vol. 17, no. 4: 447–59.

Klitgaard, R. (1995) 'Institutional Adjustment and Adjusting to Institutions', World Bank Discussion Paper no. 303, World Bank, Washington DC.

Knafo, S. (2007) 'Duménil and Lévy on Neoliberalism', *Historical Materialism*, vol. 15, no. 4: 186–94.

Konings, P. (2004) 'Opposition and Social-Democratic Change in Africa: The Social Democratic Front in Cameroon', *Commonwealth and Comparative Politics*, vol. 42, no. 3: 289–311.

Koolhaas, Rem, et al. (2000) *Mutations*, ACTAR, Barcelona.

Kothari, U. (2005) 'Authority and Expertise: The Professionalisation of Development and the Ordering of Dissent', in N. Laurie and L. Bondi (eds), *Working the Spaces of Neoliberalism*, Blackwell, Oxford: 32–54.

Kothari, U., and M. Minogue (eds) (1988) *Development Theory and Practice: Critical Perspectives*, Palgrave Macmillan, Houndmills.

Kotz, D. (2008) 'Contradictions of Economic Growth and the Neoliberal Era: Accumulation and Crisis in the Contemporary US Economy', *Review of Radical Political Economics*, vol. 40, no. 2: 174–88.

Kozul-Wright, R., and P. Rayment (2007) *The Resistible Rise of Market Fundamentalism: The Struggle for Economic Development in a Global Economy*, Zed Books, London.

Kymlicka, W. (2001) *Politics in the Vernacular: Nationalism, Multiculturalism, and Citizenship*, Oxford University Press, Oxford.

Lamont, T. (1995) 'Economic Planning and Policy Formulation in Uganda', in P. Langseth, J. Katorobo, E.A. Brett and J. Munene (eds), *Uganda: Landmarks in Rebuilding a Nation*, Fountain Press, Kampala: 11–26.

Landell-Mills, P. (1992) 'Governance, Cultural Change and Empowerment', *Journal of Modern African Studies*, vol. 30, no. 4: 543–69.

Langseth, P., and J. Mugaju (eds) (1996) *Post-conflict Uganda: Towards a Effective Civil Service*, Fountain Publishers, Kampala.

Larbi, G.A. (1995) 'The Role of Government in Adjusting Economies', Paper 2: 'Implications and Impact of Structural Adjustment on the Civil Service: The Case of Ghana', Development Administration Group, School of Public Policy, University of Birmingham.

Larner, W. (2000) 'Neoliberalism: Policy, Ideology, Governmentality', *Studies in Political Economy* 63: 5–25.

Lee, S., and S. McBride (eds) (2007) *Neoliberalism, State Power, and Global Governance*, Springer, Dordrecht.

Leys, C. (1996) *The Rise and Fall of Development Theory*, James Currey, London.

Logan, B., and D. Tevera (2001) 'Neoliberalism, Regime Survival and the Environment: Economic Reform, and Agricultural Transformation in Zimbabwe in the 1990s', *Canadian Journal of African Studies*, vol. 35, no. 1: 99–138.

Loxley, J., and H. Sackey (2008) 'Aid Effectiveness in Africa', *African Development Review*, vol. 20, no. 2: 163–99.

Lugalla, J. (1995) *Adjustment and Poverty in Tanzania*, Informationszentrum Afrika, Bremen.

McCourt, W., and M. Minogue (eds) (2001) *The Internationalisation of New Public Management*, Edward Elgar, Cheltenham.

McDonald, D., and G. Ruiters (2005) 'Theorising Water Privatisation in Southern Africa', in D. McDonald and G. Ruiters (eds), *The Age of the Commodity: Water Privatisation in Southern Africa*, Earthscan, London: 13–42.

McMichael, P. (2000) *Development and Social Change: A Global Perspective*, Pine Forge Press, Thousand Oaks CA.

Mamdani, M. (1995) 'Democratization and Marketization', in K. Mengisteab and B. Logan (eds), *Beyond Economic Liberalization in Africa*, Zed Books, London: 17–21.

Mamdani, M. (1996) *Citizen and Subject*, James Currey, London.

Manor, J. (1991) 'Politics and the Neoliberals', in C. Colclough and J. Manor (eds), *States or Markets? Neo-liberalism and the Development Policy Debate*, Clarendon, Oxford: 303–20.

Marangos, J. (2008) 'The Evolution of the Anti-Washington Consensus Debate', *Competition and Change*, vol. 12, no. 3: 227–44.

Marquette, H. (2003) *Corruption, Politics and Development: The Role of the World Bank*, Palgrave Macmillan, Basingstoke.

Marshall, J. (1990) 'Structural Adjustment and Social Policy in Mozambique', *Review of African Political Economy*, vol. 17, no. 47: 28–43.

May, R., and S. Massey (2002) 'The Chadian Party System: Rhetoric and Reality', *Democratization*, vol. 9, no. 3: 72–91.

Mbembe, A. (2001) *On the Postcolony*, University of California Press, Berkeley.

Mercer, C. (2002) 'The Discourse of *Maendeleo* and the Politics of Women's Participation on Mount Kilimajaro', *Development and Change*, vol. 33, no. 1: 101–27.

Mercer, C. (2003) 'Performing Partnership: Civil Society and the Illusions of Good Governance', *Political Geography*, vol. 22, no. 7: 741–63.

Messkoub, M. (1996) 'The Social Impact of Adjustment in Tanzania in the 1980s: Economic Crisis and Household Survival', *Internet Journal of African Studies* 1.

Milanovic, B. (2003) 'The Two Faces of Globalization: Against Globalization As We Know It', *World Development*, vol. 31, no. 4: 667–83.

Milder, D. (1996) 'Foreign Assistance: Catalyst for Domestic Coalition Building', in M. Griesgraber and B.G. Gunter (eds), *The World Bank: Lending on a Global Scale*, Pluto Press, London: 142–92.

Mkandawire, T. (1999) 'The Political Economy of Financial Reform in Africa', *Journal of International Development*, vol. 11, no. 3: 321–42.

Mkandawire, T. (ed.) (2004a) *Social Policy in a Development Context*, Palgrave Macmillan, London.

Mkandawire, T. (2004b) 'The Political Economy of the Postcolonial, Developmental State', in S. Bromley, M. Mackintosh, W. Brown and M. Wuyts (eds), *Making the International: Economic Interdependence and Political Order*, Pluto Press, London.

Mkandawire, T., and A. Olukoshi (eds) (1995) *Between Liberalisation and Oppression: The Politics of Structural Adjustment in Africa*, Council for the Development of Social Science Research in Africa (CODESRIA), Dakar.

Mohan, G., and K. Stokke (2001) 'Participation and Empowerment: The Dangers of Localism', *Third World Quarterly*, vol. 21, no. 2: 247–68.

Moore, D. (1999) '"Sail On, O Ship of State": Neoliberalism Globalisation and Governance in Africa', *Journal of Peasant Studies*, vol. 27, no. 1: 61–96.

Moore, D. (2001) 'Neoliberal Globalisation and the Triple Crisis of "Modernisation" in Africa: Zimbabwe, the Democratic Republic of Congo and South Africa', *Third World Quarterly*, vol. 22, no. 6: 909–29.

Moore, M. (1989) 'The Fruits and Fallacies of Neoliberalism: The Case of Irrigation Policy', *World Development*, vol. 17, no. 11: 1733–50.

Moore, M. (1998) 'Death without Taxes: Democracy, State Capacity, and Aid Dependency in the Fourth World', in G. White and M. Robinson (eds), *Towards a Democratic Development State*, Oxford University Press, Oxford: 84–121.

Mosley, P. (2004) 'Pro-poor Policies and the Political Economy of Stabilisation', *New Political Economy*, vol. 9, no. 2: 271–97.

Mosley, P., and J. Weeks (1993) 'Has Recovery Begun? "Africa's Adjustment in the 1980s" Revisited', *World Development*, vol. 21, no. 10: 1583–606.

Mosley, P., J. Harrigan and J. Toye (eds) (1995) *Aid and Power: The World Bank and Policy Based Lending*, Routledge, London.

Mosse, D. (2005) *Cultivating Development*, Pluto Press, London.

Mosse, D., and D. Lewis (eds) (2005) *The Aid Effect*, Pluto Press, London.

Mudimbe, V.Y. (1988) *The Invention of Africa: Gnosis, Philosophy, and the Order of Knowledge*, Indiana University Press, Bloomington.

Narayan, D., L. Pritchett and S. Kapoor (2009) *Moving Out of Poverty*, Volume 2: *Success from the Bottom Up*, Palgrave Macmillan, Houndmills.

Nares, C. (1997) *Alternative World*, Boxtree Books, London.

Nederveen Pieterse, J. (1992) *White on Black: Images of Africa in Western Popular Culture*, Yale University Press, New Haven CT.

Nederveen Pieterse, J. (2004) 'Neoliberal Empire', *Theory Culture and Society*, vol. 21, no. 3: 119–40.

Nelson, J. (ed.) (1990) *Economic Crisis and Policy Choice: The Politics of Adjustment in Developing Countries*, Princeton University Press, Princeton NJ.

Nissanke, M., and E. Thorbecke (2008) 'Globalisation – Poverty Channels and Case Studies from Sub-Saharan Africa', *African Development Review*, vol. 21, no. 1: 1–19.

Nyamugasira, W., and R. Rowden (2002) 'New Strategies, Old Loan Conditions: Do the New IMF and World Bank Loans Support Countries' Poverty Reduction Strategies? The Case of Uganda', Uganda National NGO Forum/RESULTS Educational Fund, Kampala.

Nyerere, J.K. (1974) *Man and Development*, Oxford University Press, Oxford.

O'Manique, C. (2004) *Neo-liberalism and AIDS Crisis in Sub-Saharan Africa: Globalization's Pandemic*, Palgrave Macmillan, Houndmills.

OED World Bank (2001) 'Tanzania: an Impact Evaluation of World Bank-Country Partnership in Curtailing Corruption', November, unpublished manuscript by Daniel Kobb.

Olesen, T. (2005) 'The Uses and Misuses of Globalisation in the Study of Social Movements', *Social Movement Studies*, vol. 4, no. 1: 49–63.

Ong, A. (2007a) 'Neoliberalism as a Mobile Technology', *Transactions of the Institute of British Geographers*, vol. 32, no. 1: 3–8.

Ong, C. (2007b) *Neoliberalism as Exception: Mutations in Citizenship and Sovereignty*, Duke University Press, Durham NC.

Ottaway, M. (1996) *Africa's New Leaders: Democracy or State Reconstruction?*, Carnegie Foundation, Washington DC.

Ouatarra, A. (1997) 'The Challenges of Globalization for Africa', address by Alassane D. Ouattara, deputy managing director of the International Monetary Fund, www.imf.org/external/np/speeches/1997/052197.htm, accessed March 2009.

Overbeek, H., and K. van der Pijl (1993) 'Restructuring Capital and Restructuring Hegemony', in H. Overbeek (ed.), *Restructuring Hegemony in the Global Political Economy*, Routledge, London: 1–27.

Owusu, F. (2003) 'Pragmatism and the Gradual Shift from Dependency to Neoliberalism: The World Bank, African Leaders, and Development Policy in Africa', *World Development*, vol. 31, no. 10: 1655–72.

Panitch, L., and M. Konings (2009) 'Myths of Neoliberal Deregulation', *New Left Review* 57: 67–83.

Parfitt, T. (2009) 'Are the Third World Poor *Homines Sacri*? Biopolitics, Sovereignty, and Development', *Alternatives*, vol. 34, no. 1: 41–58.

Patel, R., and P. McMichael (2004) 'Third Worldism and the Lineages of

Global Fascism: The Regrouping of the Global South in the Neoliberal Era', *Third World Quarterly*, vol. 25, no. 1: 231–54.

Peck J. (2004) 'Geography and Public Policy: Constructions of Neoliberalism', *Progress in Human Geography*, vol. 28, no. 3: 392–405.

Peck, J., and A. Tickell (2002) 'Neoliberalising Space', *Antipode*, vol. 34, no. 3: 380–404.

Peet, R. (2002) 'Ideology, Discourse, and the Geography of Hegemony: From Socialist to Neoliberal Development in Postapartheid South Africa', *Antipode*, vol. 34, no. 1: 54–84.

Peet, R. (2003) *Unholy Trinity: The IMF, World Bank and the WTO*, Zed Books, London.

Petras, J., H. Veltmeyer and L. Vasapollo (2006) *Empire with Imperialism: The Globalizing Dynamics of Neoliberal Capitalism*, Zed Books, London.

Pettifor, A., and J. Garrett (2000) 'Shadowy Figures: The G7, IMF, and World Bank – Globalisation and Debt', www.jubileeplus.org/analysis/reports/shadow0900.htm, accessed June 2003.

Phelps, N., M. Power, et al. (2007) 'Learning to Compete: Communities of Investment Promotion Practice and the Spread of Global Neoliberalism', in K. England and K. Ward (eds), *Neoliberalization: States, Networks, Peoples*, Blackwell, London: 83–109.

Picciotto, R. (1995) 'Putting Institutional Economic to Work: From Participation to Governance', World Bank Discussion Paper no. 304, World Bank, Washington DC.

Picciotto, S. (1999) 'What Rules for the World Economy?', in S. Picciotto and R. Mayne (eds), *Regulating International Business*, Palgrave, Houndmills: 1–26.

Pincus, J., and J. Winters (2003) 'Reinventing the World Bank', in J. Pincus and J. Winters (eds), *Reinventing the World Bank*, Cornell University Press, New York: 1–26.

Pinto, R. (1998) 'Innovations in the Provision of Public Goods and Services', *Public Administration and Development*, vol. 18, no. 4: 387–97.

Pitcher, M.A. (2003) *Transforming Mozambique*, Cambridge University Press, Cambridge.

Please, S. (1984) *The Hobbled Giant: Essays on the World Bank*, Westview Press, Boulder CO.

Poku, N., and A. Whiteside (eds) (2004) *The Political Economy of AIDS in Africa*, Ashgate, Aldershot.

Ponte, S. (2001) 'Trapped in Decline? Reassessing Agrarian Change and Economic Diversification on the Uluguru Mountains, Tanzania', *Journal of Modern Africa Studies*, vol. 39, no. 1: 1–24.

PORALG (2000) *Restructuring Manual*, President's Office Regional and Local Government, Dar es Salaam.

Porter, D., and D. Craig (2004) 'The Third Way and the Third World: Poverty Reduction and Social Inclusion in the Rise of "Inclusive" Liberalism', *Review of International Political Economy*, vol. 11, no. 2: 387–423.

Prempeh, E. (2006) *Against Global Capitalism: African Social Movements Confront Neoliberal Globalization*, Ashgate, Farnham.

Rakner L., and L. Svasand (2002) 'Multiparty Elections in Africa's New Democracies', *CMI Report R 2002*, C. Michelsen Institute, Bergen: 7

Rakner, L., and L. Svasand (2005) 'Stuck in Transition: Electoral Processes in Zambia 1991–2001', *Democratization*, vol. 21, no. 1: 85–105.

Rapley, J. (2002) *Understanding Development*, Lynne Rienner, Boulder CO.

Reineikka, R., and P. Collier (eds) (2001) *Uganda's Recovery: The Role of Farms, Firms, and Government*, Fountain, Kampala.

Reno, W. (2002) 'Uganda's Politics of War and Debt Relief', *Review of International Political Economy*, vol. 9, no. 3: 415–35.

Riddell, B. (1992) 'Things Fall Apart Again: Structural Adjustment Programmes in Sub-Saharan Africa', *Journal of Modern African Studies*, vol. 30, no. 1: 53–68.

Riley, S., and T. Parfitt (1994) 'Economic Adjustment and Democratization in Africa', in J. Walton and D. Seddon (eds), *Free Markets and Food Riots: The Politics of Global Adjustment*, Basil Blackwell, Oxford: 135–70.

Robison, R. (ed.) (2006) *The Neoliberal Revolution: Forging the Market State*, Palgrave Macmillan, Houndmills.

Rorty, R. (1993) 'Human Rights, Rationality, and Sentimentality', in S. Shute and S. Hurley (eds), *On Human Rights: The Oxford Amnesty Lectures 1993*, Basic Books, New York: 167–85.

Ross, M.L. (1999) 'The Political Economy of the Resource Curse', *World Politics*, vol. 51, no. 1: 297–322.

Rothchild, D. (1991) 'Introduction', in D. Rothchild (ed.), *Ghana: The Political Economy of Recovery*, Lynne Rienner, Boulder CO: 1–23.

Round, J. (2007) 'Globalisation, Growth, Inequality and Poverty in Africa', WIDER Research Paper no. 2007/55, World Institute for Development Economics Research, Helsinki.

Roy, R., A. Denzau, and T. Willett (eds) (2007) *Neoliberalism: National Experiments with Global Ideas*, Routledge, London.

Rupert, M. (2000) *Ideologies of Globalization: Contending Visions of a New World Order*, Routledge, New York.

Rye Olsen, G. (1988) 'Europe and the Promotion of Democracy in Post Cold War Africa: How Serious is Europe and for What Reason?', *African Affairs*, vol. 97, no. 388: 343–67.

Sachs, J. (2005) *The End of Poverty: How We Can Make It Happen in Our Lifetime*, Penguin, London.

Sahn, D., P. Dorosh, and S. Younger (1997) *Structural Adjustment Reconsidered*, Cambridge University Press, Cambridge.

Sandbrook, R. (1985) *The Politics of Africa's Economic Stagnation*, Cambridge University Press, Cambridge.

SAPRIN (2004) *Structural Adjustment: The Policy Roots of Economic Crisis, Poverty, and Inequality*, Zed Books, London.

Saul, J. (2005) *The Next Liberation Struggle: Capitalism, Socialism, and Democracy in Southern Africa*, Merlin Press, London.

Saunders, R. (1996) 'Zimbabwe: ESAP's Fables', *Southern Africa Report*, vol. 11, no. 2: 26–9.

Schamis, H. (1999) 'Distributional Coalitions and the Politics of Economic Reform in Latin America', *World Politics*, vol. 50, no. 2: 236–68.

Schatz, S. (1994) 'Structural Adjustment in Africa: A Failing Grade so Far', *Journal of Modern African Studies*, vol. 32, no. 4: 679–92.

Scott, J. C. (1998) *Seeing Like a State: How Certain Schemes to Improve the Human Condition Have Failed*, Yale University Press, New Haven CT.

Sender, J. (1999) 'Africa's Economic Performance: Limitations of the Current Consensus', *Journal of Economic Perspectives*, vol. 13, no. 3: 89–114.

Simon, D., W. van Spenge, C. Dixon and A. Närman (eds) (1995) *Structurally Adjusted Africa: Poverty, Debt, and Basic Needs*, Pluto Press, London.

Smith, A., A. Stenning and K. Willis (2008) *Social Justice and Neoliberalism*, Zed Books, London.

Smith, L. (2005) 'The Murky Waters of Second Wave Neoliberalism: Corporatisation as a Service Delivery Model in Cape Town', in D. McDonald and G. Ruiters (eds), *The Age of the Commodity: Water Privatisation in Southern Africa*, Earthscan, London: 168–87.

Smoke, P. (2003) 'Decentralisation in Africa: Goals, Dimensions, Myths and Challenges', *Public Administration and Development*, vol. 23, no. 1: 7–16.

Soederberg, S. (2002a) 'On the Contradictions of the New International Financial Architecture: Another Procrustean Bed for Emerging Markets?', *Third World Quarterly*, vol. 23, no. 4: 607–20.

Soederberg, S. (2002b) 'The New International Financial Architecture: Imposed Leadership and "Emerging Markets"', in L. Panitch and C. Leys (eds), *Socialist Register: A World of Contradictions*, Merlin Press, London: 175–92.

Soederberg, S. (2004) *The Politics of the New International Financial Architecture*, Zed Books, London.

Soederberg, S., G. Menz and P.G. Cerny (eds) (2005) *Internalising Globali-*

sation: The Rise of Neoliberalism and the Decline of National Varieties of Capitalism, Palgrave Macmillan, Houndmills.

Sorensen, G. (1991) 'Strategies and Structures of Development: The New "Consensus" and the Limits to Its Promises', *European Journal of Development Research*, vol. 3, no. 2: 121–45.

Steffensen, J., P. Tidemand, H. Naitore, E. Ssewankambo and E. Mwaipopo (2004) *A Comparative Analysis of Decentralisation in Kenya, Tanzania, and Uganda, Country Study: Tanzania*, NCG/Danish Trust Fund/World Bank, Dar es Salaam.

Stern, N., and F. Ferreira (1997) 'The World Bank as "Intellectual Actor"', in D. Kapur, J. Lewis, and R. Webb (eds), *The World Bank: Its First Half Century*, vol. 2, Brookings Institution Press, Washington DC: 523–609.

Stewart, F., and M. Wang (2003) 'Do PRSPs Empower Poor Countries and Disempower the World Bank, or is it the Other Way Round?', QEH Working Paper no. 108, Queen Elizabeth House (QEH), University of Oxford.

Stiglitz, J. (1999) 'Whither Reform? Ten Years of Transition', Annual Bank Conference on Development Economics, 28–30 April, World Bank, Washington DC.

Stiglitz, J. (2002) *Globalization and Its Discontents*, Allen Lane, London.

Stiglitz, J. (2007) *Making Globalization Work: The Next Steps to Global Justice*, Penguin Books, London.

Sumner, A. (2006) 'In Search of the Post-Washington (Dis)consensus: The "Missing" Content of PRSPS', *Third World Quarterly*, vol. 27, no. 8: 1401–12.

Szeftel, M. (1987) 'The Crisis in the Third World', in R. Bush, G. Johnston and D. Coates (eds), *The World Order: Socialist Perspectives*, Polity Press, Oxford: 87–141.

Takougang, J. (2003) 'The 2002 Legislative Election in Cameroon', *Journal of Modern African Studies*, vol. 41, no. 3: 421–35.

Tangri, R., and A. Mwenda (2001) 'Corruption and Cronyism in Uganda's Privatization in the 1990s', *African Affairs*, vol. 100, no. 398: 117–33.

Tangri, R., and A. Mwenda (2003) 'Military Corruption and Ugandan Politics since the late 1990s', *Review of African Political Economy*, vol. 98, no. 30: 539–52.

Taylor, L. (1997) 'The Revival of the Liberal Creed: The IMF and the World Bank in a Globalised Economy', *World Development*, vol. 25, no. 2: 145–52.

Therkilsden, O. (2000) 'Public Sector Reform in a Poor, Aid-dependent Country, Tanzania', *Public Administration and Development*, vol. 20, no. 1: 61–73.

Toussaint, E. (2008) *The World Bank: A Critical Primer*, Pluto Press, London.

Tsakalotos, E. (2004) 'Social Norms and Endogenous Preferences: The Political Economy of Market Expansion', in P. Arestis and M. Swayer (eds), *The Rise of the Market: Critical Essays on the Political Economy of Neoliberalism*, Edward Elgar, Cheltenham: 5–37.

Tsakalotos, E. (2005) 'Homo Economicus and the Reconstruction of Political Economy: Six Theses on the Role of Values in Economics', *Cambridge Journal of Economics*, vol. 29, no. 6: 983–908.

Tull, D. (2006) 'China's Engagement in Africa: Scope, Significance and Consequences', *Journal of Modern African Studies* vol. 44, no. 3: 459–79.

Turner, R. (2008) *Neoliberal Ideology*, Edinburgh University Press, Edinburgh.

UNAIDS/WHO (2003) *Aids Epidemic Update 2003*, www.unaids.org.

United Nations Expert Panel (2002) *Final Report of the Panel of Experts on the Illegal Exploitation of Natural Resources and Other Forms of Wealth of the DRC*, www.afrol.com/countries/drc/documents/un_resources_2002_intro.htm, accessed July 2003.

van de Walle, N. (2001) *African Economies and the Politics of Permanent Crisis 1979–1999*, Cambridge University Press, Cambridge.

Vlachou, A., and G. Christou (1999) 'Contemporary Economic Theory: Some Critical Issues', in A. Vlachou (ed.) *Contemporary Economic Theory: Radical Critiques of Neoliberalism*, Macmillan, Basingstoke: 1–24.

Wade, R. (2002) 'US Hegemony and the World Bank: The Fight over People and Ideas', *Review of International Political Economy*, vol. 9, no. 2: 215–43.

Wade, R. (2003) 'What Development Strategies are Viable for Developing Countries Today? The World Trade Organisation and the Shrinking of "Development" (and Democratic) Space', *Review of International Political Economy*, vol. 10, no. 4: 621–44.

Wade, R., and F. Veneroso (1998) 'The Asian Crisis: The High Debt Model vs. the Wall Street–Treasury–IMF Complex', *New Left Review*, series I, no. 228: 3–23.

Weeks, J. (2001) 'Globalize, Globa-lize, Global Lies: Myths of the World Economy in the 1990s', in R. Albritton, M. Itoh, R. Westra and A. Zuege (eds), *Phases of Capitalist Development: Booms Crises and Globalizations*, Palgrave, Houndmills: 263–83.

Weis, T. (2004) 'Restructuring and Redundancy: The Impacts and Illogic of Neoliberal Agricultural Reforms in Jamaica', *Journal of Agrarian Change*, vol. 4, no. 4: 461–91.

Weiss, B. (2004) 'Sweet Dreams: Inhabiting Masculine Fantasy in Neoliberal Tanzania', in B. Weiss (ed.), *Producing African Futures*, Brill, Leiden: 193–228.

Werbner, R., and T. Ranger (eds) (1996) *Postcolonial Identities in Africa*, Zed Books, London.

Whitfield, L. (2005) 'Trustees of Development from Conditionality to Governance: Poverty Reduction Strategy Papers in Ghana', *Journal of Modern African Studies*, vol. 43, no. 4: 641–64.

Wiegratz, J. (forthcoming) 'When you march towards market society … how changing norms, values and practices of relating and (inter-)acting in markets are reflected in forms of value chain governance', PhD, University of Sheffield.

Williams, D. (1996) 'Governance and the Discipline of Development', *European Journal of Development Research*, vol. 8, no. 2: 157–77.

Williams, D. (1999) 'Constructing the Economic Space: The World Bank and the Making of Homo Oeconomicus', *Millennium*, vol. 28, no. 1: 79–99.

Williams, D. (2008) *The World Bank and Social Transformation in International Politics: Liberalism, Governance and Sovereignty*, Houndmills, Palgrave Macmillan.

Williamson, J. (2000) 'What Should the World Bank Think about the Washington Consensus?', *World Bank Research Observer*, vol. 15, no. 2: 251–64.

Wolfson, M. (2003) 'Neoliberalism and the Social Structure of Accumulation', *Review of Radical Political Economics*, vol. 35, no. 3: 255–62.

Woodehouse, P. (2003) 'African Enclosures: A Default Mode of Development', *World Development*, vol. 31, no. 10: 1705–20.

World Bank (1981) *Accelerated Development in Sub Saharan Africa: An Agenda to Action*, World Bank, Washington DC.

World Bank (1989) *Sub-Saharan Africa: From Crisis to Sustainable Growth – a Long Term Perspective Study*, World Bank, Washington DC.

World Bank (1994a) *Adjustment in Africa: Reforms Results and the Road Ahead*, Oxford University Press, New York.

World Bank (1994b) *Governance: The World Bank's Experience*, World Bank, Washington DC.

World Bank (1995a) *The African Capacity Building Initiative: Toward Improved Policy Analysis and Development Management in Sub-Saharan Africa*, World Bank, Washington DC.

World Bank (1995b) 'Staff Appraisal Report, Republic of Uganda', Institutional Capacity Building Project Report no. 13610-UG, World Bank, Washington DC.

World Bank (1997) *World Development Report: The State in a Changing World*, Oxford University Press, Oxford.

World Bank (1999) 'Project Appraisal Document on a Proposed Credit in the Amount of SDR 29.9 Million to the United Republic of Tanzania for a Public Service Reform Project in Support of the First Phase of the Public Sector Reform Program', World Bank, Washington DC.

World Bank (2000a) *Can Africa Claim the 21st Century?*, World Bank, Washington DC.

World Bank (2000b) 'Tanzania – Accountability, Transparency and Integrity Project', Project Information Document no. PID9647, World Bank, Washington DC.

World Bank (2000c) 'Building a Tradition of Partnership and Openness: Government, Civil Society and Donors Continue Dialogue in Kampala', Presentation to Consultative Group Meeting, World Bank, Kampala.

World Bank (2000/2001) *Attacking Poverty*, Oxford University Press, New York.

World Bank (2002) *World Development Report: Building Institutions for Markets*, Oxford University Press, New York.

World Bank (2004a) 'Uganda Capacity and Performance Enhancement Programme, Project Information Document', Africa Regional Office, Report no. AB320, World Bank, Kampala.

World Bank (2004b) 'Project Appraisal Document on a Proposed Credit to the United Public of Tanzania for the Local Government Support Project', Report no. 29751–TZ, World Bank, Dar es Salaam.

World Bank (2005) *Review of World Bank Conditionality*, Operations Policy and Country Services, World Bank, Washington DC.

World Bank Public Sector Board (2000) *Reforming Public Institutions and Strengthening Governance: A World Bank Strategy*. World Bank, Washington DC.

Yeatman, A. (1990) *Bureaucrats, Femocrats, Technocrats: Essays on the Contemporary Australian State*, Allen & Unwin, Sydney.

Young, C. (2004) 'The End of the Postcolonial State in Africa? Reflections on Changing African Political Dynamics', *African Affairs*, vol. 103, no. 410: 23–51.

Zack-Williams, A. (2000) 'Social Consequences of Structural Adjustment', in G. Mohan, E. Brown, B. Milward and A. Zack-Williams, *Structural Adjustment: Theory Practice, and Impacts*, Routledge, London: 59–74.

Index